AWS Certified SysOps Administrator Associate Practice Tests

250 AWS Practice Exam Questions with Answers

Nicola Erbacci

Introduction

The world has changed drastically over the years. Just 50 years ago, it would have seemed impossible to think that the vast majority of things would come to be done through the internet, which at that time existed as a research project. It would have seemed absurd to think at that time that all the daily processes could be done from a mobile phone, but today that seems completely normal. The internet has completely revolutionized our lives and has fostered modernization and globalization, which has helped us evolve in leaps and bounds.

Even the most complex tasks can be carried out online. Best of all, it is said that the internet and technology are not even close to their limits, so there is still a long way to go. Within all this change, one of the things that has most evolved is the business world. Thanks to the internet, businesses move very differently from how they used to. We have many tools that allow us to carry out processes and tasks much more easily.

Within this evolution, many new jobs require extensive technical knowledge, as well as skills related to innovation and programming. Decades ago, there were no community managers, web developers, online consultants, or any of the professions that rely on the technological advances of the online world. Today, each of those jobs may be vital for the operation and success of a large company.

Some companies have sprung up to make things easier for consumers and even for other companies. One of these companies is Amazon, which has grown from a bookseller to providing global access to quickly buy anything from anywhere. However, Amazon has expanded to many other services based in media and technology. People can develop professional careers and make a lot of money based solely on Amazon services. One of those opportunities is to become AWS SysOps Administrator. AWS is a cloud service, with all that entails. Development is one of the most promising professions, and certification shows prospective employers that you know your stuff and can help them reach maximum potential.

To become an AWS SysOps Administrator, one must take a test that requires a lot of preparation and knowledge to pass. This book is going to prepare you in the best way for this test, by reviewing some of the most common questions that may appear in these tests, the test format, and some tips that will help you get the highest possible score.

Many people believe that passing these exams is difficult. You must have a lot of general programming knowledge and, of course, knowledge of Amazon's computing services. The test requires preparation and extensive knowledge. It requires that you apply concentration, discipline, and perseverance as you study to reach your goal of becoming an AWS SysOps Administrator.

This test is ideal for all those with one or more years of hands-on experience developing and maintaining an AWS-based application. It is recommended that you have certain skills and knowledge before you take the exam, such as in-depth knowledge of at least one high-level programming language, a grasp of the core AWS services, and enough basic understanding of cloud-native applications to write code. Each of these skills is easy to learn, but you must master them to pass the test. Many people attempt the test without being fully prepared, which is not only a waste of time and money but also often serves to demotivate them and to make them believe that this is not the right way to go. But if you have mastered these skills and do your best to absorb the information in this book, there is no doubt that you can achieve excellent results.

It is recommended that you have a pencil and a notebook at hand as you read so that you can write down all the data, questions, and tips that you find interesting. Of course, you will not be able to use these notes during the exam, but they will help you study and prepare.

You must also make sure that this is your true passion, so that you are motivated to take this exam and obtain the best possible grades. Many people want to obtain the certificate so that they will have more job opportunities and more chances of having a successful programming career. However, anyone who does this solely for money and not because they are truly passionate about the work will find the path to success difficult. If, on the other hand, you are passionate about these types of services, you know how to use most of the applications, you have experience, and you know what you can achieve with the certification, then start preparing for this exam and for reaching your goals. If you are ready to start your journey through the world of AWS, you are in the right place.

1. AWS CloudTrail logs must be secured by a SysOps Administrator. The Security team is concerned that an employee could change or remove CloudTrail log files from the company's Amazon S3 bucket. Which procedures guarantee that log files are accessible and unaltered? (Select two.)

   A. In AWS Config Rules, enable the CloudTrail log file integrity check.

   B. Scanning log files hourly with CloudWatch Events.

   C. Turn on CloudTrail log file integrity checking.

   D. For the CloudTrail bucket, enable Amazon S3 MFA Delete.

   E. On the CloudTrail bucket, create a DENY ALL bucket policy.

2. A corporation runs a web application that people can access by typing www.example.com into their browser. Amazon Route 53 is used to manage the domain name. The corporation put an Amazon CloudFront distribution in front of the app and wants www.example.com to be able to access it through CloudFront. What is the most cost-effective method of accomplishing this?

   A. In Amazon Route 53, create a CNAME record that points to the CloudFront distribution URL.

   B. In Amazon Route 53, create an ALIAS record that points to the CloudFront distribution URL.

   C. Create an A record in Amazon Route 53 that points to the web application's public IP address.

   D. Create a PTR record in Amazon Route 53 that links to the web application's public IP address.

3. A corporation that uses AWS Organizations must never delete any Amazon S3 buckets in its production accounts. What is the most straightforward way a SysOps Administrator may do to ensure that S3 buckets in those accounts are never deleted?

    A. Enable MFA Delete on all S3 buckets to prevent them from being removed accidentally.

    B. Deny the s3:DeleteBucket operation on all buckets in production accounts using service control policies.

    C. Create an IAM group with an IAM policy that prevents all buckets in production accounts from using the s3:Delete-Bucket action.

    D. Instead of all S3 buckets, use AWS Shield to deny the s3:Delete-Bucket operation on the AWS account.

4. For its apps, a corporation employs numerous accounts. Account A is in charge of the Amazon Route 53 domains and hosted zones for the company. The company's web servers are fronted by a load balancer in Account B. What is the most cost-effective and efficient way for the organization to use Route 53 to point to the load balancer?

    A. In Account A, create an Amazon EC2 proxy that redirects requests to Account B.

    B. In Account A, create a load balancer that refers to the load balancer in Account B.

    C. Create a CNAME record in Account A that points to an alias record in Account B for the load balancer.

    D. In Account A, create an alias record that points to the load balancer in Account B.

5. A SysOps Administrator receives notification that a security vulnerability exists in a version of MySQL utilized by Amazon RDS MySQL. Who is in charge of ensuring the patch is installed on the MySQL cluster?

    A. The database vendor

    B. The Security department of the SysOps Administrator company

    C. Amazon Web Services

    D. The SysOps Administrator

6. Behind an ELB Application Load Balancer, a company's web application runs on Amazon EC2 instances. The EC2 instances are distributed across several Availability Zones in an EC@ Auto Scaling group. An Amazon ElastiCache for Redis cluster and an Amazon RDS DB instance hold the data. All system patches must be completed by Tuesday midnight, according to company policy. Which resources will require a maintenance window set for Tuesday at midnight? (Select two.)

    A. Elastic Load Balancer

    B. EC2 instances

    C. RDS instance

    D. ElastiCache cluster

    E. Auto Scaling group

7. A SysOps Administrator is putting dynamic content on a website. Users from particular countries or areas are prohibited from accessing site material and should receive an error page, according to company policy. Which of the following methods can be utilized to put this policy into effect? (Select two.)

    A. Geo-restriction on Amazon CloudFront

    B. Geo-blocking using Amazon GuardDuty

C. Amazon Route 53 geolocation routing

D. Geo-restriction of AWS Shield

E. Restriction on the network access control list (NACL)

8. A corporation uses an Amazon S3 bucket to store thousands of non-critical log files. These log files are retrieved daily by a series of reporting routines. For the company's use case, which of the following storage alternatives will be the MOST cost-effective?

A. Amazon Glacier

B. Standard IA (infrequent access) storage on Amazon S3.

C. Standard Amazon S3 Storage

D. AWS Snowball

9. When using SSH to connect to an Amazon EC2 instance from a home network, a SysOps Administrator receives a connection timeout problem. In the past, the Administrator was able to SSH into this EC2 instance from their office network. What is the cause of the connection timeout?

A. The SSH connections from the home network are not allowed by the IAM role associated with the EC2 instance.

B. The SSH public key on the Administrator's server does not have the necessary permissions.

C. In the VPC's route table, there is a route that sends 0.0.0.0/0 to the internet gateway.

D. On the SSH port, the security group is blocking inbound traffic from the home network.

10. A corporation is using an Elastic Load Balancer to deploy a web service to Amazon EC2 instances. All resources will be defined and created using a template in a single AWS CloudFormation stack. The creation of each EC2 instance will not be considered complete until the instance's startup script has been completed successfully. After all EC2 instances have been created, the Elastic Load Balancer may be created. In the CloudFormation stack template, which CloudFormation resource will coordinate the Elastic Load Balancer creation?

    A. CustomResource

    B. DependsOn

    C. Init

    D. WaitCondition

11. An organization is concerned about a security flaw in their Linux operating system. What can the SysOps Administrator do to address this issue?

    A. Use Amazon Inspector to fix the issue.

    B. Provide a report from AWS Trusted Advisor indicating which Amazon EC2 instances have been patched.

    C. Using AWS CloudFormation, re-deploy the Amazon EC2 instances.

    D. Use AWS Systems Manager to patch the Linux operating system.

12. For the first time, a SysOps Administrator is configuring AWS SSO. The Administrator has already used AWS Directory Service to build a directory in the master account and enabled full access in AWS Organizations. When it comes to configuring the service, what should the Administrator do next?

A. Create IAM roles in each account that will be utilized by AWS SSO, then use AWS SSO to associate users with these roles.

B. In the master account, create IAM users and use AWS SSO to link the users to the accounts they'll be accessing.

C. In AWS SSO, create permission sets and associate them with Directory Service users or groups.

D. In Organizations, create service control policies (SCPs) and associate them with Directory Service users or groups.

13. A web application that accesses external services operates on Amazon EC2 instances. Authentication credentials are required by external services. The application is deployed to three different environments using AWS CloudFormation: development, test, and production. Each environment has its own set of authentication services. What solution securely gives the required credentials to the application with the least amount of administrative overhead?

A. As arguments, pass the target environment's credentials to the CloudFormation template. To inject parameterized credentials into EC2 instances, utilize the user data script.

B. Save the credentials in the AWS Systems Manager Parameter Store as secure strings. The CloudFormation template accepts an environment tag as a parameter. To add the environment tag to the EC2 instances, utilize the user data script. The credentials can be accessed through the application.

C. For each environment, create a separate CloudFormation template. Include a user data script for each EC2 instance in the Resources section. Use the user data script to populate the EC2 instances with the appropriate environment credentials.

D. For each environment, create distinct Amazon Machine Images (AMIs) with the needed credentials. The environment tag should be passed to the CloudFormation template as a parameter. Map the environment tag to the right AMI in the

CloudFormation template's Mappings section, then use that AMI when launching the EC2 instances.

14. For the first time, a SysOps Administrator generated an AWS CloudFormation template. With a status of ROLLBACK COMPLETE, the stack failed. The failure was caused by a template issue, which was found and rectified by the Administrator. How should the stack deployment be continued by the Administrator?

    A. Remove the failed stack and replace it with a fresh one.

    B. Run a change set on the stack that failed.

    C. On the unsuccessful stack, perform an update-stack operation.

    D. Use the validate-template command to validate the template.

15. A SysOps Administrator is developing a procedure for exchanging Amazon RDS database snapshots amongst accounts connected with different business units within the same organization. At rest, all data must be encrypted. How should the Administrator go about putting this system in place?

    A. Create a script to download the encrypted snapshot, decrypt it if necessary using the AWS KMS encryption key, and then create a new volume in each account.

    B. Update the key policy to grant all applicable accounts access to use the AWS KMS encryption key used to encrypt the snapshot, then share the snapshot with them.

    C. Create an Amazon EC2 instance based on the snapshot, then save and share the snapshot of the instance's Amazon EBS volume with the other accounts. Require each account owner to build and encrypt a new volume from the snapshot.

    D. From the encrypted snapshot, create a new unencrypted RDS instance and connect to it through SSH/RDP. The contents of the database should be exported to a file, which should then be shared with the other accounts.

16. A SysOps Administrator has been notified that a vulnerable software version may be deployed on some Amazon EC2 instances in the company's environment. What should be done to check all instances in the environment with the least amount of operational overhead?

    A. Make an Amazon Inspector assessment template and run it.

    B. Check the software version by manually SSHing into each instance.

    C. Verify Amazon EC2 activities in the account using AWS CloudTrail.

    D. Create a custom script and deploy it to Amazon EC2 instances using AWS CodeDeploy.

17 Several workloads are maintained on AWS by development teams. Concerned about escalating expenditures, company management has asked the SysOps Administrator to set up alerts so that teams are notified when spending reaches predefined limits. Which AWS service will meet these criteria?

    A. Budgets of Amazon Web Services

    B. AWS Cost Explorer

    C. AWS Trusted Advisor

    D. AWS Cost and Usage report

18. A SysOps Administrator is responsible for delivering and managing a single CloudFormation template across numerous Amazon Web Services accounts. What AWS CloudFormation function will help you achieve this?

    A. Change sets

    B. Nested stacks

    C. Stack policies

    D. StackSets

19. A corporation runs a MySQL-based application on Amazon RDS. The Development team found a considerable increase in query latency during load testing of equal production volumes. The CPU utilization on the RDS MySQL instance was at 100%, according to Amazon CloudWatch Logs, according to a SysOps Administrator. What is the best course of action for resolving this problem?

    A. Enable Amazon RDS for MySQL to scale and accept more queries by configuring AWS Database Migration Service (AWS DMS).

    B. To offload write requests, configure RDS for MySQL to scale horizontally by adding more nodes.

    C. For the RDS instance, enable the Multi-AZ functionality.

    D. Change the instance type of the RDS MySQL instance to a larger one.

20. In a company's AWS environment, a SysOps Administrator encrypts an Amazon EBS volume using AWS KMS and AWS-generated key material. The Administrator wishes to use automatic key rotation to rotate the KMS keys and verify that the EBS disk encrypted with the current key is still readable. What needs to be done in order to achieve this?

    A. Create a backup of your current KMS key and turn on automatic key rotation.

    B. In AWS KMS, create a new key and assign it to Amazon EBS.

    C. In AWS KMS, enable automatic key rotation for the EBS volume key.

    D. In AWS KMS, upload new key material to the EBS volume key to allow automatic key rotation.

21. An AWS Elastic Beanstalk worker node environment was created by a SysOps Administrator that reads messages from an auto-generated Amazon Simple Queue Service (Amazon SQS) queue and deletes them after processing. The number of worker nodes in Amazon EC2 Auto Scaling is scaled in and out based on CPU utilization. After some time, the Administrator observes a large increase in the number of messages in the SQS queue. What is the best course of action for resolving this problem?

   A. Modify the scaling policy such that it scales according to the number of messages in the queue.

   B. Create a separate resource for the queue and decouple it from the Elastic Beanstalk worker node.

   C. Increase the queue's amount of messages.

   D. Make the queue's retention period longer.

22. A security team is concerned about the possibility of confidential information spilling onto the internet. The objective of a SysOps Administrator is to find controls to solve the potential problem. The servers in question are housed in a virtual private cloud (VPC) and are not permitted to transfer traffic to the internet. What is the best way to meet these requirements?

   A. Make the following change to the subnet's route:

      – Destination 0.0.0.0/0

      – target: igw-xxxxxxxx

   B. Check to see if the servers have Elastic IP addresses.

   C. To regulate traffic flows, enable Enhanced Networking on the instances.

   D. Create a private subnet for the servers.

23. A business is establishing a VPC peering link between its VPC and that of a customer. The customer's VPC has an IPv4 CIDR block of 10.0.0.0/16, whereas the companies has an IPv4 CIDR block of 172.16.0.0/16. From one of the company's Amazon EC2 instances, the SysOps Administrator wishes to be able to ping the customer's database private IP address. What steps should be made to ensure that the requirements are met?

A. To construct a file sharing network, first ensure that both accounts are linked and that they are part of consolidated billing, and then activate VPC peering.

B. Make sure both VPC owners manually add a route to their VPC route tables that points to the other VPC's IP address range.

C. Tell the customer to create a VPC with the same 172.16.0.0/16 IPv4 CIDR block as the source VPC.

D. Assign the customer the task of creating a virtual private gateway to connect the two VPCs.

24. Because all of its Amazon EC2 instances are housed in a single Amazon VPC in us-east-1, a corporation is concerned about its capacity to recover from a disaster. In eu-west-1, a second Amazon VPC has been configured to operate as a backup VPC in the event of an outage. The primary region's data will be duplicated to the secondary region. All data must be encrypted and must not pass through the public internet, according to the Information Security team's compliance criteria. What should the SysOps Administrator do to join the two VPCs while being compliant?

A. Set up EC2 instances as VPN appliances, and then set up route tables.

B. Configure route tables after configuring inter-region VPC peering between the two VPCs.

C. In both VPCs, configure NAT gateways before configuring route tables.

D. In each VPC, set up an internet gateway and use it as the target for the VPC route tables.

25. Two companies will collaborate on a number of development projects. Each company has an AWS account in us-east-1 with a single VPC. Two businesses want to use each other's development servers. There is no overlap between the IPv4 CIDR blocks in the two VPCs. What can each company's SysOps Administrators do to build up network routing?

    A. Each Administrator should develop a custom routing table that points to the public IP address of the other company's internet gateway.

    B. In their respective VPCs, both Administrators should set up a NAT gateway in a public subnet. The Administrators should then enable routing between the two VPCs using the public IP address from the NAT gateway.

    C. In their respective environments, both Administrators should install a 1 Gbps AWS Direct Connect circuit. The Administrators should then use the AWS Management Console to issue an AWS Direct Connect routing request to enable connectivity.

    D. Create a VPC peering request in one Administrator's account and submit it to the other Administrator's account. Update the routing tables to enable traffic after the other Administrator accepts the request.

26. A SysOps Administrator is in charge of keeping an Amazon EC2 instance that serves as a bastion host up and running. The Administrator may connect to the instance through SSH without issue, but attempts to ping the instance fail due to a timeout. What is one possible cause of the problem?

   A. The instance lacks an Elastic IP address.
   B. The instance is protected by a security group that blocks Internet Control Message Protocol (ICMP) communication.
   C. The instance is not connected to an AWS Direct Connect VPC.
   D. The instance is running in a VPC with many peers.

27. According to a Common Vulnerabilities and Exposures (CVE) report, a number of Amazon EC2 instances in a VPC are marked as high risk by an enterprise organization. All of these instances should be upgraded, according to the security team. Who is in charge of the EC2 instances' upgrades?

   A. The Amazon Web Services Security team
   B. The Amazon EC2 team B. The Amazon EC2 team
   C   The Amazon Web Services Premium Support team
   D. The Systems Administrator for the company

28. An Amazon CloudFront web distribution, an Application Load Balancer (ALB), Amazon RDS, and Amazon EC2 in a VPC are used by a SysOps Administrator to operate a web application. Logging is enabled for all services. The web application's HTTP Layer 7 status codes must be investigated by the Administrator. What are the log sources where the status codes can be found? (Select two.)

   A. VPC Flow Logs
   B. Amazon Web Services CloudTrail logs
   C. ALB access logs
   D. CloudFront access logs
   E. RDS logs

29. A corporation must make sure that all IAM users' passwords are rotated on a regular basis. What steps should be made to put this into action?

    A. Make sure that all IAM users have multi-factor authentication enabled.

    B. Every time a credential rotation is required, deactivate existing users and create new users.

    C. Every time a credential rotation is required, recreate identity federation with new identity providers.

    D. Set up a password policy to enable password expiration for IAM users.

30. Behind an Application Load Balancer, an application operates on Amazon EC2 instances (ALB). The instances are part of an Auto Scaling group that terminates any instances that are unhealthy. The Auto Scaling group is set up to use both EC2 status checks and ALB health checks to determine the health state of EC2 instances. Before terminating, the Development team wishes to investigate the harmful cases. To achieve this, what should the SysOps Administrator do?

    A. Instead of terminating instances, configure the ALB health check to restart them.

    B. Set up an AWS Lambda code to take a snapshot of all instances before they're shut down.

    C. Use Amazon CloudWatch Events to gather lifecycle events and activate a remediation AWS Lambda function.

    D. After an instance has been removed from service, use an Amazon EC2 Auto Scaling lifecycle hook to stop instance termination.

31. To access a database, an Amazon EC2 application requires login credentials. The login credentials are saved as secure string parameters in the AWS Systems Manager Parameter Store. What is the SAFEST approach to provide the application access to your credentials?

    A. For the EC2 instances, create an IAM EC2 role and provide it permission to read the Systems Manager parameters.

    B. Assign the application to an IAM group and provide the group authorization to view the Systems Manager parameters.

    C. For the application, create an IAM policy and grant it permission to read the Systems Manager parameters.

    D. Assign the application to an IAM user and provide the user permission to read the Systems Manager parameters.

32. A SysOps Administrator is receiving notifications about a Memcached-based Amazon ElastiCache cluster's high CPU use. What actions should be performed to remedy this problem? (Select two.)

    A. Increase the size of the Amazon EBS volume on the ElastiCache cluster nodes.

    B. Add a load balancer to the ElastiCache cluster to route traffic

    C. Add more worker nodes to the ElastiCache cluster

    D. Add an Auto Scaling group to the ElastiCache cluster

    E. Change the node type 33 to vertically scale the ElastiCache cluster.

33. An Amazon RDS MySQL DB instance in production is managed by a SysOps Administrator. Several apps make use of the database. In the event that the database fails, the Administrator must guarantee that the applications experience minimal downtime. During regular business hours, this change must not affect customer use. Which activity will increase the database's availability?

A. Contact AWS Support to have the database pre-warmed so that it can manage any traffic spikes that may occur.

B. Create a new Multi-AZ RDS Database instance.

C. Create a read replica from the existing database hours Migrate the data to the new DB instance and destroy the old one

D. Make the DB instance a Multi-AZ deployment outside of business hours.

34. The AWS Management Console is accessed over federated Security Assertion Markup Language (SAML). What is the best way to set up the SAML assertion mapping?

A. Associate the group attribute with an Amazon Web Services group. IAM policies that regulate access to AWS resources are allocated to the AWS group.

B. Associate the policy attribute with the IAM policies that the federated user belongs to. Access to AWS resources is governed by these policies.

C. Assign the role attribute to an Amazon Web Services role. IAM policies that regulate access to AWS resources are allocated to the AWS role.

D. Associate the user attribute with an AWS account. IAM policies that regulate access to AWS resources are assigned to each AWS user.

35. Behind an ELB Application Load Balancer, a SysOps Administrator manages a web application that operates on Amazon EC2 instances (ALB). An EC2 Auto Scaling group is used to run the instances. When all target instances linked with the ALB are unhealthy, the administrator wants to issue an alarm. Which condition should the alarm be set to?

    A. AWS/ApplicationELB HealthyHostCount <= 0

    B. AWS/ApplicationELB UnhealthyHostCount >= 1

    C. AWS/EC2 StatusCheckFailed <= 0

    D. AWS/EC2 StatusCheckFailed >= 1

36. A NAT instance has been set up to allow web servers to download software updates from the internet. As the network increases, the NAT instance has a lot of latency. A SysOps Administrator must reduce instance latency in a way that is efficient, cost-effective, and enables for future demand scalability. What steps should be done to achieve this?

    A. Create a second NAT instance and put both behind a load balancer.

    B. Increase the instance size of the NAT instance.

    C. Use a NAT gateway instead of a NAT instance.

    D. Use a virtual private gateway to replace the NAT instance.

37. A new Common Vulnerabilities and Exposures (CVE) report affecting a major operating system has been published by a security researcher. The latest CVE report has disturbed a SysOps Administrator, who wants to patch the company's systems as soon as possible. The administrator contacts Amazon Web Services (AWS) and requests that the fix be applied to all Amazon EC2 instances. How will Amazon Web Services reply to this request?

    A. During the next maintenance window, AWS will deploy the patch and provide the Administrator with a report of all patched EC2 instances.

B. AWS will relaunch the EC2 instances with the most recent Amazon Machine Image (AMI) and send the Administrator a report of all patched EC2 instances.

C. AWS will investigate the vulnerability to see if it affects the Administrator's operating system, and will patch any vulnerable EC2 instances.

D. AWS will discuss the shared responsibility model with the Administrator and provide instructions on how to patch the EC2 instances.

38. A web application's development team recently published a new version to production. Penetration testing identified a cross-site scripting vulnerability after the release, which might expose user data. Which AWS service will help you solve this problem?

A. Amazon Web Services Shield Standard

B. Amazon Web Services WAF

C. Elastic Load Balancing

D. Amazon Cognito of Amazon Web Services

39. A development team is working on a hybrid deployment application that processes sensitive data. The team must guarantee that the data in the application is secure both in transit and at rest. Which actions should be conducted in what order to achieve this? (Select two.)

A. Create a tunnel between the on-premises data center and the AWS resources using a VPN.

B. Create TLS/SSL certificates with AWS Certificate Manager.

C. Encrypt the data with AWS CloudHSM.

D. Create TLS/SSL certificates with AWS KMS.

E. Manage the encryption keys used for data encryption with AWS KMS.

40. AWS Storage Gateway is being used by a corporation to construct block storage volumes from on-premises servers and mount them as Internet Small Computer Systems Interface (iSCSI) devices. Some Development teams indicate that the performance of the iSCSI disks has decreased as the Storage Gateway has taken on multiple additional projects. A SysOps Administrator observes that the CacheHitPercent metric is below 60% and the CachePercentUsed metric is above 90% when looking at Amazon CloudWatch metrics. What actions should the administrator take to improve the performance of the Storage Gateway?

A. To boost I/O speed, increase the default block size for the Storage Gateway from 64 KB to 128 KB, 256 KB, or 512 KB.

B. Make the cached volume's disk larger. Edit the local disks in the AWS Management Console, then choose the new disk as the cached volume.

C. To increase throughput, make sure the Storage Gateway's physical disks are configured in RAID 1.

D. Take point-in-time snapshots of all volumes in Storage Gateway, completely flush the cache, and then restore the volumes from the clean snapshots.

41. On an Application Load Balancer, a SysOps Administrator notices a high amount of malicious HTTP requests (ALB). Various IP addresses are used to make the requests. What should be done to stop this flow of people?

A. Use Amazon CloudFront to cache traffic and prevent bots and scrapers from accessing your web servers.

B. Use Amazon Guard Duty to defend your web servers from bots and scrapers.

C. Analyze web server logs with AWS Lambda, detect bot traffic, and block IP addresses in security groups using AWS Lambda.

D. When traffic surpasses a certain threshold, use AWS WAF rate-based blacklisting to block it.

42. A business has provided SSL certificates to its customers and must ensure that the private keys used to sign the certificates are encrypted. The business must be able to securely store private keys and perform cryptographic signature operations. To achieve these needs, what service should be used?

    A. Amazon Web Services CloudHSM

    B. Amazon Web Services KMS

    C. Amazon Web Services Certificate Manager

    D. Amazon Connect

43. A SysOps Administrator is attempting to set up an Amazon Route 53 domain name to route traffic to an Amazon S3-hosted website. www.anycompany.com is the website's domain name, and anycompany-static is the S3 bucket. The domain name www.anycompany.com does not appear to work once the record set is created in Route 53, and the static website does not appear in the browser. Which of the following is the root of the problem?

    A. The S3 bucket must first be configured using Amazon CloudFront.

    B. The Route 53 record set must have an IAM role that permits access to the S3 bucket.

    C. The S3 bucket and the Route 53 record set must be in the same region.

    D. The name of the S3 bucket must be the same as the Route 53 record set.

44. An ecommerce company's SysOps Administrator notices that a single IP address is receiving several 404 errors every minute. The Administrator believes a bot is collecting data from the company's website's product listings. Which service should be utilized to detect and block this potentially harmful activity?

    A. AWS CloudTrail

    B. Amazon Inspector

    C. AWS Shield Standard

    D. AWS WAF

45. A company wants to reduce costs across the entire company after discovering that several Amazon Web Services accounts were using unauthorized services and incurring extremely high costs. Which AWS service enables the company to reduce costs by controlling access to AWS services for all Amazon Web Services accounts?

    A. Amazon Web Services Cost Explorer

    B. Amazon Web Services Config

    C. Amazon Web Services Organizations

    D. Amazon Web Services Budgets

46. On Amazon RDS, a corporation performs a resource-intensive reporting task that uses an application database. Other apps that rely on the database are experiencing performance issues as a result of this. What actions should the SysOps Administrator take to remedy this problem?

    A. Make backups on Amazon RDS.

    B. To execute the report, set up Amazon RDS read replicas.

    C. Turn on Amazon RDS's Multi-AZ mode.

    D. Make use of Amazon RDS's host replacement service.

47. A corporation wishes to improve the availability and long-term viability of a mission-critical application. A MySQL database on an Amazon EC2 instance is currently used by the application. The firm wishes to keep application changes to a minimum. What is the best way for the business to meet these demands?

A. The EC2 instance should be shut down. Start the EC2 instance after enabling multi-AZ replication.

B. Run MySQL on a secondary EC2 server, and set up a cron job to back up the database on the first EC2 instance every 30 minutes and copy it to the secondary instance.

C. Create a Read Replica in a different Availability Zone and migrate the database to an Amazon RDS Aurora DB instance.

D. Create a Microsoft SQL Database instance on Amazon RDS and activate multi-AZ replication. Back up the old database and import it into the new one.

48. An AWS CloudFormation template of the company's existing infrastructure in us-west-2 is owned by a SysOps Administrator. The Administrator tries to utilize the template to start a new stack in eu-west-1, but the stack only deploys partially, then rolls back after receiving an error notice. What are the chances that this template won't work? (At least two options are available.)

A. The template made a reference to an IAM user that isn't present in eu-west-1.

B. The template used an Amazon Machine Image (AMI) that was not available in the eu-west-1 region.

C. The template's permissions were insufficient to deploy the resources.

D. The template requested services that eu-west-1 does not provide.

E. Only existing services can be updated using CloudFormation templates.

49. For a new AWS account, a SysOps Administrator must establish user-defined cost allocation tags. For account management, the company employs AWS Organizations. What should the Administrator do to allow users to create their own cost allocation tags?

    A. Create new user-defined cost allocation tags using the Cost Allocation Tags manager in the AWS Billing and Cost Management console of the new account.

    B. Use the Cost Allocation Tags manager to generate the new user-defined cost allocation tags in the AWS Billing and Cost Management dashboard of the payer account.

    C. Log in to the new account's AWS Management Console, use the Tag Editor to generate new user-defined tags, and then mark the tags as cost allocation tags using the new account's Cost Allocation Tags manager.

    D. Log into the new account's AWS Management Console, utilize the Tag Editor to generate new user-defined tags, and then mark the tags as cost allocation tags in the payer account's Cost Allocation Tags Manager.

50. A corporation created a memory-intensive application that is now running on numerous Amazon EC2 Linux instances. Every minute, the memory usage metrics of the EC2 Linux instances must be checked. What is the best way for a SysOps Administrator to report memory metrics? (At least two options are available.)

    A. In Amazon CloudWatch, turn on detailed monitoring for the instance.

    B. Disseminate the memory measurements through Amazon CloudWatch Events.

    C. Use Amazon CloudWatch to publish memory metrics.

    D. Using Amazon CloudWatch Logs, publish the memory measurements.

    E. Make the metrics collection interval 60 seconds long.

51. An organization is launching a new static website on Amazon S3. The bucket's static website hosting option was enabled, and content was uploaded, but when you go to the site, you get the following error message: Access Denied: 403 Forbidden What should be changed to correct the problem?

A. Create a bucket policy that gives everyone in the bucket read access.

B. Include a bucket policy that allows everyone to read the bucket objects.

C. Disable the bucket's default read-only policy.

D. On the bucket, enable CORS (cross-origin resource sharing).

52. An Amazon RDS MySQL DB instance is being used by a business. A daily database backup must be replicated to a separate security account, according to corporate policy. What is the MOST cost-effective method of meeting this requirement?

A. Using the AWS CLI and the copy-db-snapshot command, copy an automatic RDS snapshot to the security account.

B. For the essential database in the security account, create an RDS MySQL Read Replica and activate automatic backups for the Read Replica.

C. Using the AWS CLI's create-db-snapshot command, generate an RDS snapshot, share it with the security account, and then duplicate it in the security account.

D. Replicate data from the crucial database to another RDS MySQL instance in the security account using AWS DMS, then backup the RDS instance using an automatic backup.

53. When total billing for all AWS accounts within an organization reaches a specific amount, a SysOps Administrator must set up notifications. AWS Organizations and Consolidated Billing have been activated by the Administrator. To set up the billing alerts, what further steps does the Administrator need to take?

    A. In the payer account, enable billing alerts in the Billing and Cost Management interface, and when the billing alert is triggered, send an Amazon SNS message.

    B. In each account, enable billing alerts in the Billing and Cost Management console, create a billing alarm in Amazon CloudWatch, and send an SNS message when the alarm goes off.

    C. In the payer account, enable billing alerts in the Billing and Cost Management console, and set up a billing alarm in the Billing and Cost Management console to send an SNS message when the alarm goes off.

    D. In the payer account, enable billing alerts in the Billing and Cost Management console; create a billing alarm in Amazon CloudWatch; and send an SNS message when the alarm goes off.

54. A VPN connects a virtual private cloud (VPC) to a corporate data center. A private subnet of the VPC is home to an Amazon EC2 instance with the IP address 172.31.16.139. An on-premises computer with the IP address 203.0.113.12 sent a ping instruction to the EC2 instance, but received no response. The VPC Flow Logs were turned on, and the following information was displayed:

    What action will resolve the issue?

    2 123456789012 eni-1234bca 203.0.113.12 172.31.16.139 0 0 1 4 336 1432917027 1432917142 ACCEPT OK

    2 123456789012 eni-1234bca 172.31.16.139 203.0.113.12 0 0 1 4 336 1432917027 1432917142 ACCEPT OK

A. Change the EC2 security group rules to allow traffic from the on-premises PC to flow in.

B. Change the EC2 security group rules so that outbound traffic to the on-premises computer is allowed.

C. Change the ACL rules on the VPC network to enable inbound traffic from the on-premises machine.

D. Add outbound traffic to the on-premises machine to the VPC network ACL rules.

55. Behind an ELB Application Load Balancer, a web application is hosted on Amazon EC2 instances. Multiple Availability Zones are accessible to instances in an EC2 Auto Scaling group. The load balancer is served by Amazon Route 53, which is utilized for DNS. A SysOps Administrator has created a new Auto Scaling group with a fresh version of the application and want to progressively migrate traffic to it. What's the best way to do it?

A. Create an Auto Scaling target tracking scaling strategy to progressively migrate traffic from the old to the new version.

B. Switch the Application Load Balancer to a Network Load Balancer, then add both Auto Scaling groups as targets.

C. Use an Route 53 weighted routing policy to gradually move traffic from the old to the new version

D. Deploy Amazon Redshift to gradually migrate traffic from the old to the new version using a set of predefined values

56. Users are authenticated and AWS rights are granted using federation. AWS Organizations has asked the SysOps Administrator to figure out who requested a new AWS account. What should the Administrator look at in order to figure out who submitted the request?

A. Amazon Web Services CloudTrail for the federated identity user name

B. Amazon Web Services IAM Access Advisor for the federated user name

C. Amazon Web Services Organizations access log for the federated identity user name

D. Federated identity provider logs for the user name

57. A serverless application powered by AWS Lambda should see a considerable rise in traffic. The Lambda function must be set to scale for the application to handle the increasing traffic, according to a SysOps Administrator. What actions should the Administrator take in order to achieve this goal?

A. Add more elastic network interfaces to the Lambda function

B. Set up Amazon Web Services Application Auto Scaling for the number of invocations depending on the Amazon CloudWatch Lambda metric

C. Make sure the Lambda function's concurrency limit is larger than the predicted simultaneous function executions

D. Make the Lambda function's memory more available.

58. An Amazon EC2 instance has ceased responding, and a SysOps Administrator is contacted. System checks are failing, according to the AWS Management Console. To remedy this problem, what should the SysOps Administrator do first?

    A. Restart the EC2 instance on a new host.

    B. Shut down and restart the EC2 instance so that it can be moved to a new host.

    C. Shut down and restart your EC2 instance.

    D. Look at the AWS CloudTrail log to see what happened with the EC2 instance.

59. To maintain session state for a web application and to cache frequently used data, an ecommerce site uses Amazon ElastiCache with Memcached. Users have been expressing dissatisfaction with performance over the last month. The metrics for the Amazon EC2 and Amazon RDS instances look to be normal, however the eviction count numbers are abnormally high. What should be done to resolve this problem and boost productivity?

    A. Add more nodes to the cluster to increase its size.

    B. Add read replicas to the cluster to scale it up.

    C. Scale the cluster by increasing CPU capacity

    D. Scale the web layer by adding extra EC2 instances

60. An on-premises asymmetric key management system must be migrated to Amazon Web Services (AWS). To do this, which AWS service should be used?

    A. Amazon Web Services Certificate Manager

    B. Amazon Web Services CloudHSM

    C. Amazon Web Services KMS

    D. Amazon Web Services Secrets Manager

61. A SysOps Administrator is setting up a test site that will run on Amazon EC2 instances. The application necessitates Internet connectivity on both an incoming and outgoing basis. To enable internet access to the EC2 instances, what procedures must be taken in which order? (At least two options are available.)

A. Add a NAT gateway to a public subnet

B. Attach a private address to the elastic network interface on the EC2 instance

C. Give your internet gateway an Elastic IP address.

D. Create a route entry for the subnet that points to an internet gateway in the route table.

E. Set up an internet gateway and connect it to a virtual private network (VPC).

62. An Amazon EC2 workload is being examined for prohibited AMI usage by a security and compliance team. A SysOps Administrator should recommend which course of action.

A. Use AWS Systems Manager Inventory to create a custom report that identifies AMIs that aren't allowed.

B. Run Amazon Inspector on all EC2 instances, flagging those that use unapproved AMIs.

C. To detect unapproved AMIs, use an AWS Config rule.

D. Identify EC2 workloads running unapproved AMIs using AWS Trusted Advisor.

63. A business must have real-time access to picture data while still preserving an offsite copy of the photographs. Which AWS solution would provide both local access to the image data and catastrophe recovery?

A. Create a volume gateway configured as a stored volume in AWS Storage Gateway. The Internet Small Computer System Interface is used to mount it from clients (iSCSI).

B. Use a local server to mount an Amazon EFS volume. Employees that require access to the images should share this volume.

C. Upload the photos to Amazon S3 and utilize AWS Data Pipeline to cache S3 data locally.

D. To improve local speed, utilize Amazon S3 for file storage and enable S3 Transfer Acceleration to keep a cache of frequently used files.

64. In a new AWS account, a SysOps Administrator must replicate a company's existing AWS infrastructure. At the moment, resources are created and managed using an AWS Service Catalog portfolio. What is the MOST EFFECTIVE method of achieving this?

A. To use the AWS Service Catalog portfolio in the new AWS account, first create an AWS CloudFormation template.

B. Duplicate the old portfolio by manually creating an AWS Service Catalog portfolio in the new AWS account.

C. Using the output of the DescribePortfolio API action, use the AWS Lambda function to establish a new AWS Service Catalog portfolio.

D. Distribute the AWS Service Catalog portfolio to other AWS accounts and import it into other accounts.

65. Using AWS Organizations, a corporation manages multiple accounts under a single umbrella. Some employees are abusing AWS services, according to the Security team. A SysOps Administrator must block all account users from executing certain restricted tasks, including the root user. What needs to be done in order to achieve this?

   A. Use service control policies (SCPs) to only allow allowed actions.

   B. Use service control policies (SCPs) to keep restricted actions from happening.

   C. Establish permissions boundaries so that only authorized actions are permitted.

   D. Establish permissions boundaries to avoid limiting actions.

66. Behind an Application Load Balancer, an application runs on Amazon EC2 instances (ALB). A set of Amazon EC2 Auto Scaling instances has been created. The program must be scaled dependent on the volume of incoming requests, according to a SysOps Administrator. Which solution takes the least amount of time and effort to complete?

   A. Implement a simple scaling policy based on a custom metric that calculates the average active requests across all EC2 instances.

   B. Apply a straightforward scaling policy based on the GroupDesiredCapacity metric from the Auto Scaling group.

   C. Implement a target tracking scaling policy based on the ActiveConnectionCount metric from the ALB.

   D. Scale target tracking using the ALB's RequestCountPerTarget measure

67. In the us-east-1 Region, a SysOps Administrator has used an AWS CloudFormation template to build an Amazon EC2 instance. This template failed to establish an EC2 instance in the us-west-2 Region, as discovered by the Administrator. What do you think one of the reasons for this failure could be?

    A. The CloudFormation template's resources tags are unique to the us-east-1 Region.

    B. In the us-west-2 Region, the Amazon Machine Image (AMI) ID given in the CloudFormation template was not discovered.

    C. During resource provisioning in the us-west-2 Region, the cfn-init script failed to execute.

    D. In the selected Region, the IAM user was not created.

68. Users are having difficulty connecting to a single public-facing development web server through its public IP address and a single port number of 8181. The security group is set up properly to enable access to that port, and the network ACLs are set up as they should be. Which log type will show whether people are attempting to connect to the proper port?

    A. Logs from AWS CloudTrail

    B. Logs of access to the Elastic Load Balancer

    C. VPC Flow Logs

    D. Access logs from Amazon S3

69. AnyCompany's security team uncovers that some workers are utilizing AWS accounts that are not within the company's control. Individual accounts have been requested to be linked to the central company utilizing AWS Organizations, according to the team. To accomplish this, what should a SysOps Administrator do?

   A. Using Amazon Web Services IAM, add each existing account to the central organization.

   B. In each account, create a new organization and link it to the main one.

   C. Log into each existing account and link it to the central organization.

   D. The central organization should send each existing account an invitation.

70. A SysOps Administrator has been tasked with enabling access logging for a Network Load Balancer and is creating an Amazon S3 bucket to store the logs. What are the S3 bucket's bare minimum requirements? (At least two options are available.)

   A. The bucket and the Network Load Balancer must be in the same Region.

   B. The bucket must have a bucket policy allowing Elastic Load Balancing to write access logs to it.

   C. Encryption should be enabled in the bucket.

   D. Lifecycle policies must be set in the bucket.

   E. Public access to the bucket must be turned off.

71. An Amazon EC2 instance hosts an application. The application's access to an Amazon S3 bucket must be granted by a SysOps Administrator. What can be done to ensure the highest level of security?

    A. Create an S3 bucket policy that allows all EC2 instances to access the bucket.

    B. Make an IAM user and a script to insert credentials at boot time.

    C. For Amazon S3 access to the EC2 instance, create and assign an IAM role.

    D. Inside the Amazon Machine Image, embed an AWS credentials file for an IAM user (AMI).

72. A company's marketing department generates and keeps gigabytes of assets every day. They want to back up the files to Amazon Web Services (AWS) to protect them. Although all materials should be kept on the cloud, the most recent ones should be accessible locally for low latency access. Which AWS service is the best fit for your needs?

    A. Amazon EBS

    B. Amazon EFS

    C. Amazon S3

    D. Amazon Web Services Storage Gateway

73. A SysOps Administrator is attempting to utilize AWS Systems Manager Session Manager to establish an SSH session with an Amazon EC2 instance running on a custom Linux Amazon Machine Image using AWS Systems Manager Session Manager (AMI). The target instance in the Session Manager console cannot be found by the Administrator. Which set of actions will be most effective in resolving the problem? (At least two options are available.)

A. In the instance profile, add permissions for Systems Manager.

B. Allow write access to the bucket used by the Session Manager logs.

C. Set up the instance with the Systems Manager Agent.

D. Allow inbound traffic on SSH port 22 by changing the instance security group.

E. Restart the instance using the ssm-user SSH key pair.

74. The AWS Storage team expects all data transfers to an Amazon S3 bucket to stay within the AWS network. All AWS network infrastructure upgrades are made manually by the team. An S3 VPC endpoint is built, as well as an endpoint policy with appropriate rights. The S3 bucket endpoint is still unavailable to the application operating on Amazon EC2 instances in the VPC. What could be a contributing factor to this problem?

A. The S3 bucket's request metrics must be turned on.

B. For the VPC endpoints to function, S3 access logs must be disabled.

C. The VPC endpoint is not listed in the subnet's route table as a target.

D. An Elastic Network Adapter must be enabled in the EC2 instances.

75. An IAM policy is developed and associated to an IAM role as part of a federated identity configuration. According to the shared responsibility paradigm, who is accountable for developing an IAM policy and linking it to an IAM role?

   A. AWS is in charge of developing the IAM policy for the role and attaching it to it.

   B. The position is created by AWS, and the policy is attached to the role by a SysOps Administrator.

   C. The IAM policy is created and attached to the role by a SysOps Administrator.

   D. The role must be created by a SysOps Administrator, and the policy must be attached by AWS.

76. Behind an Application Load Balancer, an application is hosted on Amazon EC2 instances (ALB). Across several Availability Zones, the instances run in an Auto Scaling group. The Information Security team wishes to keep track of application requests by originating IP and EC2 instance. Which of the following tools or services can you use to get this data?

   A. Amazon CloudWatch

   B. Amazon Web Services CloudTrail

   C. ELB access logs

   D. VPC Flow Logs

77. Data must be copied to an Amazon S3 bucket by an Amazon EC2 instance running in a private subnet. The connection between the EC2 instance and Amazon S3 should not cross the Internet for security reasons. What is the best course of action for the SysOps Administrator to pursue in order to achieve this?

A. Set up a NAT instance and use it to direct traffic to Amazon S3.

B. Connect the EC2 instance to Amazon S3 using a VPN.

C. In the VPC where the EC2 instance is running, create an S3 VPC endpoint.

D. To boost throughput while keeping traffic secret, use AWS Direct Connect.

78. An AWS Storage Gateway is being set up by a SysOps Administrator. When the Administrator uses the Storage Gateway console to activate the Storage Gateway, it fails. What could be the root of the problem? (At least two options are available.)

A. No upload buffer is configured on the Storage Gateway.

B. An Amazon S3 bucket for backup is not configured on the Storage Gateway.

C. A cache volume is not configured on the Storage Gateway.

D. The time is incorrect on the Storage Gateway.

E. The Administrator's client cannot access the Storage Gateway over port 80.

79. A SysOps Administrator must keep track of all of an Amazon S3 bucket's object upload and download activity. The caller's AWS account, IAM user role, the time of the API call, and the API's IP address must all be tracked during monitoring. What information is available to the Administrator?

A. Amazon Web Services CloudTrail data event logging

B. Amazon Web Services CloudTrail management event logging

C. Amazon Inspector bucket event logging

D. Amazon Inspector user event logging

80. For several hours, a company's website was unavailable. A full disk on one of the company's Amazon EC2 instances was the root cause. Which actions should the SysOps Administrator take to ensure that this does not happen again?

A. Use Amazon CloudWatch Events to filter and forward AWS Health events about disk space use to an Amazon SNS topic, which will alert the Administrator.

B. Create an Amazon Web Services Lambda function to describe each EC2 instance's volume status. When a volume status is impaired, send a notification to an Amazon SNS topic.

C. Make thorough monitoring of the EC2 instances possible. Create an Amazon CloudWatch alarm to alert the Administrator when disk space is low.

D. Collect disk metrics using the Amazon CloudWatch agent on the EC2 instances. Create a CloudWatch alarm to alert the Administrator when disk space is low.

81. A SysOps Administrator needs to get a file from Amazon S3's GLACIER storage class. When the file becomes ready for download, the Administrator wishes to be notified via Amazon SNS. What steps should be made to achieve this goal?

A. Using the GlacierJobDescription API, create an Amazon CloudWatch Events event for file restoration from Amazon S3 Glacier and deliver the event to an SNS topic that the Administrator has subscribed to.

B. Create an AWS Lambda function that conducts a HEAD request on the item to be restored and checks the object's storage class. When the storage class changes to STANDARD, send a notification to an SNS topic to which the Administrator has subscribed.

C. For the s3, enable an Amazon S3 event notification:The ObjectCreated:Post event sends a notification to an Administrator-subscribed SNS topic.

D. Enable S3 event notification for the s3:ObjectCreated:Completed event, which sends a notification to an SNS topic subscribed to by the Administrator.

82. One of a company's Amazon EBS-backed Amazon EC2 instances is on hardware that is scheduled for maintenance, according to its AWS Personal Health Dashboard. The instance is used to handle a mission-critical production workload that must be available during regular business hours. Which actions will ensure that instance maintenance does not result in a service interruption?

A. Create an Amazon Lambda function to start the instance automatically if it is stopped.

B. Create an Amazon Machine Image (AMI) of the instance and use it to start a new instance after the old one is shut down.

C. On the EC2 instance, enable termination protection.

D. During a maintenance window outside of usual business hours, stop and restart the EC2 instance.

83. Security has detected an IP address that should be explicitly blocked for all services in an Amazon VPC for both ingress and egress requests immediately. Which feature can be used to fulfill this need?

A. Firewalls that are based on the host

B. NAT Gateway

C. Lists of network access control

D. Security Groups

84. In front of Amazon EC2 instances, an Application Load Balancer (ALB) is set up. The current health check setting for the target group is as follows: 30 second interval Threshold for being unhealthy: ten Healthy criterion: 5 What should a SysOps Administrator do to shorten the time it takes to eliminate unhealthy instances? (Select two.)

    A. Change the configuration of the healthy threshold to 1.

    B. Increase the interval setting to 15.

    C. Increase the number of intervals to 60.

    D. Increase the unhealthy threshold setting to 15.

    E. Set the unhealthy threshold to 5.

85. A company has a web application that is used by all departments of the organization. The name of the division making the request is included in the header of each application request. Each division's requests should be identified and counted, according to the SysOps Administrator. To accomplish this, which condition should be added to the AWS WAF's web ACL?

    A. Cross-site scripting (XSS) is a type of cross-site scripting that allows

    B. Geographical compatibility

    C. IP compatibility

    D. String similarity

86. A SysOps Administrator is deploying an Amazon EC2 instance and routing traffic to an on-premises data center using third-party VPN software. According to the shared responsibility paradigm, AWS is in charge of which aspect of this deployment?

    A. Setting up the VPN's Ipsec tunnels.

    B. Assuring the EC2 instance's high availability.

    C. Ensuring that the VPN connection is always available.

    D. Maintaining the underlying EC2 host's health.

87. An automated failover of an Amazon RDS database is reported to a SysOps Administrator. What could be the reason of this? (Select two.)

   A. The database is experiencing read contention.

   B. The primary database suffers from a storage failure.

   C. A database with a write contention.

   D. Errors in the database.

   E. The type of database instance has been changed.

88. A recent AWS CloudFormation stack update failed, and the error UPDATE ROLLBACK FAILED was returned. The CloudFormation stack must be restored to its prior functional state by a SysOps Administrator. What must be done in order to achieve this?

   A. Correct the error that caused the rollback to fail, then utilize the console to select the Continue Update Rollback option.

   B. In the console, select the Update Stack action with a working template.

   C. Change the IAM user's password, then choose the Continue Update Rollback action in the console.

   D. Change the stack status to UPDATE COMPLETE using the AWS CLI, then continue updating the stack using a functional template.

89. A corporation needs to operate a distributed application across numerous Amazon EC2 instances to analyze a huge amount of data. The application is built to withstand disruptions in processing. For these needs, what is the most cost-effective Amazon EC2 pricing model?

   A. Committed Hosts

   B. Instances on Demand

   C. Reserved Instances

   D. Identifying Instances

90. An Amazon EC2 instance's clock was misconfigured by one hour by a SysOps Administrator. Through the CloudWatch agent, the EC2 instance sends data to CloudWatch. The logs' timestamps are 45 minutes in the future. What will be the outcome of this set-up?

   A. Because the data is in the future, Amazon CloudWatch will not capture it.

   B. Amazon CloudWatch will accept and record the custom metric data.

   C. Before transferring the data, the Amazon CloudWatch agent will check the Network Time Protocol (NTP) server and fix the time.

   D. The Amazon CloudWatch agent will check the Network Time Protocol (NTP) server, but the data will not be sent because the time is more than 30 minutes away.

91. A corporation just conducted a security audit of all of its in-house created internal apps. Because they use Amazon ES clusters that are available for read/write to a wider user group than intended, several business-critical apps that handle sensitive data have been highlighted. Who is in charge of resolving the problem?

   A. AWS Premium Support

   B. the ES team at Amazon

   C. AWS Identity and Access Management team

   D. SysOps Administrator

92. For the Operations team, a SysOps Administrator has created a new Amazon S3 bucket named mybucket. Members of the team are members of an IAM group that has been assigned the following IAM policy:

On the bucket, which of the following acts will be permitted? (Select two.)

   A. Get the bucket region.

   B. Remove an object from the scene.

   C. Delete the bucket.

   D. Get a hold of a file.

   E. Make a list of all of the account's buckets.

93. Access to an Amazon S3 bucket must be limited to Amazon EC2 instances within a VPC. The AWS private network must be used for all traffic. What steps should the SysOps Administrator take to ensure that these standards are met?

   A. For the S3 bucket, construct a VPC endpoint and an IAM policy that conditionally limits all S3 actions on the bucket to the VPC endpoint as the source.

   B. For the S3 bucket, construct a VPC endpoint and an S3 bucket policy that conditionally limits all S3 activities on the bucket to the VPC endpoint as the source.

   C. Create an Amazon EC2 service-linked role that allows EC2 instances to interface directly with Amazon S3, as well as an IAM policy that grants full access to the S3 bucket to the EC2 instances.

   D. In the VPC, set up a NAT gateway and change the VPC route table to send all traffic to Amazon S3 through the NAT gateway.

94. Using Cost Explorer, a Chief Financial Officer has requested a breakdown of costs per project in a single AWS account. To achieve this, what combination of options should be selected? (Select two.)

A. Turn on AWS Budgets.

B. Make the cost allocation tags active.

C. Use AWS Organizations to create an organization.

D. Make resource tags and use them.

E. Make AWS Trusted Advisor available.

95. A SysOps Administrator has created a VPC network design that satisfies the following criteria:

– 2 Availability Zones

– 2 private subnets

– 2 public subnets

– 1 internet gateway

– 1 NAT gateway

What would potentially cause applications in the VPC to fail during an AZ outage?Because it can only be coupled with a single AZ, A. A single virtual private gateway.

A. A single virtual private gateway, because it can be associated with a single AZ only.

B. Because it is not redundant across both AZs, a single internet gateway is used.

C. Because it is not redundant across both AZs, a single NAT gateway is used.

D. The default VPC route table, which can only be connected with one AZ.

96. An application that maintains a configuration file in an Amazon S3 bucket is supported by a SysOps Administration team. For change control and rollback, previous revisions of the configuration file must be kept. To meet these needs, how should the S3 bucket be configured?

    A. On the S3 bucket, enable a lifecycle policy.

    B. On the S3 bucket, enable cross-origin resource sharing.

    C. On the S3 bucket, enable item tagging.

    D. On the S3 bucket, enable versioning.

97. A corporation has an established web application that runs across two Availability Zones on two Amazon EC2 instances behind an Application Load Balancer (ALB). An Amazon RDS Multi-AZ DB Instance is used by the application. Requests for dynamic content are routed to the load balancer, while requests for static material are routed to an Amazon S3 bucket. Visitors to the site are complaining about unusually slow loading times. What steps should be performed to improve the website's performance? (Select two.)

    A. For static material, enable Amazon CloudFront caching.

    B. Switch the HTTPS listener on the load balancer to TCP.

    C. Enable latency-based routing on Amazon Route 53.

    D. For the web servers, use Amazon EC2 Auto Scaling.

    E. Transfer static content from Amazon S3 to web servers.

98. AWS is being used to migrate an application with the requirement that archived data be kept for at least 7 years. To achieve this compliance need, which Amazon Glacier configuration option should be used?

    A. A policy for retrieving data from Glacier

    B. A policy for gaining access to the Glacier vault

    C. A policy for securing the vaults at Glacier National Park

    D. Notification of a Glacier Vault

99. A corporation has numerous AWS accounts and has used AWS Organizations to set up consolidated billing. Over the course of several months, the total monthly bill has risen, and a SysOps Administrator has been tasked with determining what is causing this rise. What is the MOST COMPREHENSIVE tool for achieving this goal?

    A. Amazon Web Services Cost Explorer

    B. Amazon Web Services Trusted Advisor

    C. Tags for cost allocation

    D. Collaborative groupings

100. AWS CloudFormation was used to deploy a company's infrastructure. The infrastructure was recently changed manually by the company. The duty of determining what changed and changing the CloudFormation template falls to a SysOps Administrator. Which solution will guarantee that all modifications are recorded?

    A. Based on the modifications made, create a new CloudFormation stack. Delete the old stack and replace it with the new one.

    B. Use a change set to update the CloudFormation stack. Examine the modifications and make any necessary updates to the stack.

    C. Update the CloudFormation stack by changing the template's selected parameters to match the changes.

    D. On the CloudFormation stack, use drift detection. Update the CloudFormation template and redeploy the stack using the output.

101. A file was accidentally removed from an Amazon EBS volume by a user. The volume's SysOps Administrator discovered a recent snapshot. What should the Administrator do if the user's file from the snapshot needs to be restored?

    A. Copy the destroyed file to a new Amazon EC2 instance in the same Availability Zone as the snapshot.

    B. Navigate to the snapshot and copy the file to an Amazon EC2 instance's EBS disk.

    C. From the snapshot, create a volume, attach it to an Amazon EC2 instance, and copy the deleted file.

    D. Using the Amazon EC2 console, restore the file from the snapshot to an EC2 instance.

102. A company's SysOps Administrators each have their own IAM user account. Each user belongs to the SysOps IAM group, which has an IAM policy in place. Employees must now utilize their on-premises Active Directory user accounts to access the AWS Management Console, according to a recent update to the IT security policy. To meet these requirements, which solution should be used?

    A. Set up AWS Direct Connect in your on-premises Active Directory.

    B. In an Amazon Route 53 private zone, enable Active Directory federation.

    C. Configure an Active Directory connector and set up a VPN tunnel.

    D. For IAM and Active Directory, use multi-factor authentication.

103. A firm needs to install a web application behind an Application Load Balancer on two Amazon EC2 instances (ALB). The database will be hosted on two EC2 instances as well. The infrastructure must be configured for high availability across Availability Zones, and public access to instances must be limited as much as feasible. What is the best way to accomplish this within a VPC?

   A. Create three public subnets: one for the Application Load Balancer, one for the web servers, and one for the database servers.

   B. Set up one public subnet for the Application Load Balancer, two public subnets for web servers, and two private subnets for database servers.

   C. Split the Application Load Balancer into two public subnets, two private subnets for the web servers, and two private subnets for the database servers.

   D. Separate the Application Load Balancer into two public subnets, the web servers into two public subnets, and the database servers into two public subnets.

104. AWS sends an email to a SysOps Administrator about a production Amazon EC2 instance backed by Amazon EBS that is on a degraded host that is soon to be retired. The planned retirement occurs during important business hours. What should be done to ensure that the business is not disrupted as much as possible?

   A. Before the scheduled retirement, reboot the instance as soon as feasible to undertake system maintenance.

   B. Perform system maintenance before the scheduled retirement by rebooting the instance outside of business hours.

   C. Move to a new host before the scheduled retirement by stopping/starting the instance outside of business hours.

   D. Create an AWS Lambda function to restore the system when it is time for it to retire.

105. A business application is hosted on Amazon EC2 instances and is protected by an Application Load Balancer. The CPU use on the EC2 instances is very high, according to Amazon CloudWatch measurements. When users try to connect to the application, they obtain HTTP 503 and 504 problems, according to reports. Which course of action will be most effective in resolving these problems?

A. Create an AWS Auto Scaling group for the EC2 instances.

B. Change the Target Group of the ALB to use more regular health checks.

C. On the Application Load Balancer, enable sticky sessions.

D. Increase the Application Load Balancer's idle timeout setting.

106. Behind an Application Load Balancer, a SysOps Administrator manages an application that operates on Amazon EC2 instances (ALB). When attempting to activate the application, users are encountering difficulties. The HTTPCode ELB 5xx Count Amazon CloudWatch statistic for the load balancer has increased, according to the Administrator. What could be the reason for this rise?

A. Within the VPC, the ALB is linked to private subnets.

B. A client sent a request to the ALB, but the client terminated the connection.

C. The ALB security group is not set up to accept users' inbound traffic.

D. There are no healthy EC2 instances in the ALB target group.

107. Currently, an application is running on many Amazon EC2 instances within a VPC. The EC2 instances are unable to access the public internet due to compliance limitations. To perform maintenance and other administrative activities, SysOps Administrators require SSH access to EC2 instances from their corporate headquarters. Which actions should be made in which order to provide SSH access to the EC2 instances while remaining compliant? (Select two.)

    A. Connect the VPC to a NAT gateway and set up routing.

    B. Connect the VPC to a virtual private gateway and set up routing.

    C. Connect the VPC to the internet and set up routing.

    D. Set up a virtual private network (VPN) connection to the corporate office.

    E. In front of the EC2 instances, set up an Application Load Balancer.

108. A developer is implementing a web application behind an Application Load Balancer (ALB) on Amazon EC2 instances and observes that the application is not receiving all of the required components from HTTP requests. Users may not be delivering the correct query string, according to the developer. What should a sysops administrator do to double-check this?

    A. Keep an eye on the default Amazon CloudWatch metrics for ALB. Check to see if the requests have the expected query string.

    B. set up the ALB so that access logs are stored in Amazon S3. Check that the query string in the log entries is what you anticipate.

    C. Go to Amazon CloudWatch and open the ALB logs. Check to see if requests have the expected query string.

    D. To store requests, create a custom Amazon CloudWatch measure. Check to see if the metric has the expected query string.

109. The IT department of a corporation saw an increase in the amount of money spent on their Developer AWS account. The account is used by over 50 Developers, and the Finance team needs to see how much each one is spending on service. What should a SysOps Administrator do in order to gather this data? (Select two.)

    A. Enable the account's created By tag.
    B. Enable the use of Amazon CloudWatch dashboards.
    C. Use Cost Explorer to examine the consumption.
    D. Use AWS Trusted Advisor to keep track of your resource utilization.
    E. In AWS Budgets, set up a billing alarm.

110. For in-memory caching of popular product queries on the shopping site, an ecommerce company utilizes an Amazon ElastiCache for Memcached cluster. The sysops administrator detects a huge number of evictions when looking at recent Amazon CloudWatch metrics data for the ElastiCache cluster. Which of the following actions is most likely to reduce evictions? (Select two.)

    A. Add an additional node to the ElastiCache cluster
    B. Increase the ElastiCache time to live (TTL)
    C. Increase the individual node size within the ElastiCache cluster
    D. Place an Elastic Load Balancer in front of the ElastiCache cluster E. Decouple the ElastiCache cluster

111. using Amazon Simple Queue Service (Amazon SQS). Within a VPC with no Internet connectivity, a sysops administrator developed an AWS Lambda function. The Lambda function retrieves messages from an Amazon SQS queue and saves them to an Amazon RDS instance in the same VPC. The data does not appear on the RDS instance after executing the Lambda function. Which of the following could be the reason for this? (Select two.)

A. For Amazon RDS, no VPC endpoint has been configured.

B. For Amazon SQS, no VPC endpoint has been setup.

C. Connections from the Lambda function are denied by the RDS security group.

D. There is no internet gateway attached to the Lambda function's subnet.

E. There is a NAT gateway attached to the Lambda function's subnet.

112. For its Data Scientists, a corporation created a custom Amazon EC2 instance configuration. The Data Scientists want to be able to create and delete EC2 instances on their own, but they aren't sure how to configure all of the settings for EC2 instances without help. The setup runs proprietary software that must be kept secret within the company's AWS accounts and should only be accessible by Data Scientists and no other users. Which solution should a SysOps Administrator utilize to allow Data Scientists to deploy workloads with the least amount of effort possible?

A. Make an AMI (Amazon Machine Image) of the EC2 instance. Share the AMI with the company's authorized accounts. Allow the Data Scientists to use this AMI to construct EC2 instances.

B. From an Amazon S3 bucket, distribute an AWS CloudFormation template with the EC2 instance configuration to the Data Scientists. Set the orgId of the AWS Organizations to read the S3 template object.

C. In the Private Marketplace, publish the instance settings. Share the company's AWS accounts with the Private Marketplace. Allow Data Scientists to subscribe to the Private Marketplace and launch the offering.

D. In the AWS Service Catalog, upload an AWS CloudFormation template. Allow Data Scientists to provision and deprovision goods from the AWS Service Catalog portfolio of the firm.

113. A corporation created a memory-intensive application, which it now runs on several Amazon EC2 Linux instances. The memory use metrics of the EC2 Linux instances must be kept track of. Which steps must be completed in what order to achieve this? (Select two.)

    A. In Amazon CloudWatch, enable comprehensive monitoring for the instance.

    B. Track memory metrics with an AWS Lambda function.

    C. To track memory metrics, install the Amazon CloudWatch agent.

    D. Make the memory measurements available through Amazon CloudWatch Events.

    E. Use Amazon CloudWatch Logs to publish the RAM measurements.

114. A SysOps Administrator has been asked to create an additional environment for an application in four additional regions by an Application team. In us-east-1, the application is running on over 100 instances utilizing fully baked AMIs. To deploy resources in us-east-1, an AWS CloudFormation template was constructed. What should the SysOps Administrator do to get the application up and running quickly?

    A. Using aws ec2 copy-image, copy the AMI to each region. Include mappings for the cloned AMIs in the CloudFormation mapping.

    B. Make a copy of the running instance's snapshot and paste it into the other areas. From the pictures, create an AMI. To use the updated AMI, update the CloudFormation template for each region.

    C. Based on the success of the template used in us-east-1, run the existing CloudFormation template in each additional region.

    D. Update the CloudFormation template to include the Auto Scaling group's additional regions. In us-east-1, update the existing stack.

115. A firm wants to know which Amazon EC2 instances are underutilized and how much money they may save each instance. How can this be accomplished with the bare minimum of effort?

    A. Use AWS Budgets to report on low EC2 instance use.

    B. Check for low memory use of EC2 instances using an AWS Systems Manager script.

    C. Use Cost Explorer to hunt for EC2 instances that are underutilized.

    D. Identify EC2 instances with low utilization using Amazon CloudWatch measurements.

116. A SysOps Administrator must manage access to Amazon EC2 instance groups. On the EC2 instances, specific tags have already been inserted. What further steps should the Administrator take to keep access under control? (Select two.)

    A. Assign an IAM policy to the users or groups who require EC2 instance access.

    B. Assign an IAM role to the EC2 instances to control access.

    C. Assign a specific tag to the EC2 instances and create a placement group for them.

    D. Make a service account and link it to the EC2 instances you want to manage.

    E. Create an IAM policy that allows any EC2 instance with a tag specified in the Condition element to access it.

117. In the eu-west-1, ap-east-1, and us-west-1 Regions, a corporation intends to launch various ecommerce websites. Amazon S3 buckets, Amazon EC2 instances, Amazon RDS databases, and Elastic Load Balancers make up the websites. Which technique will require the LEAST amount of effort to complete the deployment?

    A. Set up AWS OpsWorks for deployment automation.

    B. Set up cross-region replication in S3.

C. Deploy the application using AWS CloudFormation stack settings.

D. Deploy the application using AWS Elastic Beanstalk.

118. A firm controls numerous AWS accounts and wants to give access to AWS using an existing on-premises Microsoft Active Directory domain. Which method requires the LEAST amount of effort to achieve these requirements?

   A. Using AWS Directory Service, create an Active Directory connector. Create IAM users with the appropriate trust policy in the target accounts.

   B. Using AWS Directory Service, create an Active Directory connector. Connect the directory to the AWS Single Sign-On service (AWS SSO). AWS SSO is used to grant users access to target accounts.

   C. Create a federated identity pool in Amazon Cognito. Associate the pool identification with the directory on the premises. Configure the proper trust policy for the IAM roles.

   D. Connect the on-premises directory to an identity provider in AWS IAM. Create IAM roles with the appropriate trust policy in the target accounts.

119. A corporation has multiple AWS accounts for different departments and wants to simplify billing and cut costs. The organization wants to make sure that the finance team can't access anything but Amazon EC2, that the security team can't access anything but AWS CloudTrail, and that IT can access anything. Which option has the LEAST amount of operational overhead and meets these requirements?

   A. Within AWS IAM, create a role for each department and assign each role the relevant rights.

   B. Within AWS IAM, create a user for each department and provide each user the relevant permissions.

C. Within AWS Organizations, implement service control policies to establish which resources each department has access to.

D. Within AWS Organizations, group each department into an organizational unit (OU) and use IAM policies to specify which resources they have access to.

120. A corporation uses a serverless architecture to run an image-processing application. A single AWS Lambda execution is used for each processing job. Even if additional Lambda functions are running for other applications, a sysops administrator must ensure that there is enough capacity to handle 500 simultaneous jobs. Within the Region, the administrator has already increased service limits. What is the best course of action?

A. Create a dead-letter queue to allow throttled executions to be retried.

B. Change the Lambda function's memory parameters to allow for 500 concurrent runs.

C. Use AWS Step Functions to handle image processing.

D. Set the image-processing Lambda function's reserved concurrency to 500.

121. An AWS Lambda function is used by a sysops administrator to execute maintenance on multiple AWS services. This function needs to be executed every night. Which option is the most cost-effective?

A. Create a single t2.nano Amazon EC2 instance and a Linux cron job to call the Lambda function every night at the same time.

B. Create an Amazon CloudWatch metrics alarm to run the Lambda function every night at the same time.

C. Create a CloudWatch event to call the Lambda function every night at the same time.

D. Create a Chef recipe in the AWS OpsWorks stack to call the Lambda function every night at the same time.

122. A sysops administrator is managing an application on AWS that uses Amazon EC2 instances and Amazon Aurora MySQL. The EC2 instances and Aurora instances are in two different subnets. The application servers running in EC2 cannot connect to the Aurora database. The EC2 subnet is 192.168.87.0/24 and has a security group named sg-123456 with the following configuration.

Inbound rules
Protocol type Port Number Source IP
TCP 22 (SSH) 192.168.87.0/24
ICMP All 0.0.0.0/0

Outbound rules
Protocol type Port Number Destination IP
All All 0.0.0.0/0

The Aurora subnet is 192.168.88.0/24 and has a security group named sg-abcdef with the following configuration.

Inbound rules
Protocol type Port Number Source IP
MYSQL/Aurora 3306 192.168.88.0/24

Outbound rules
Protocol type Port Number Destination IP
All All 0.0.0.0/0

To allow the EC2 instances to connect to the Aurora database, what action should the sysops administrator take?

A. Add an incoming TCP rule with the MySQL port and sg-123456 as the traffic source to the Aurora security group's inbound rules database.

B. Add an incoming TCP rule with the MySQL port and 192.168.88.0/24 as the traffic source to the EC2 security group's inbound rules table.

C. In the Aurora security group's outbound rules table, create an outbound TCP rule with the MySQL port as the source and 192.168.87.0/24 as the destination.

D. In the EC2 security group's outbound rules table, add an outbound TCP rule with the MySQL port as the source and sg-abcdef as the destination.

123. A multi-tier web application is used by a firm. All of the servers in the web tier are in private subnets within a VPC. The application's development team needs to make some changes that require access to Amazon S3. What needs be done in order to achieve this?

A. To connect to Amazon S3, create a customer gateway. To use the customer gateway, change the route table of the private subnets.

B. Create an Amazon S3 gateway VPC endpoint. To use the gateway VPC endpoint, change the route table of the private subnets.

C. In the private subnets, set up a NAT gateway. Change the subnets' route tables to use the NAT gateway.

D. Create an S3 bucket policy that allows private subnet connections. Make changes to the route table.

124. A sysops administrator is in charge of a VPC network that includes both public and private subnets. A NAT gateway connects instances in private subnets to the Internet. The NAT gateway charges have increased, according to a recent AWS bill. The administrator needs to know which instances are causing the greatest traffic on the network. What is the best way to go about doing this?

A. Enable flow logging on the NAT gateway's elastic network interface and filter data using Amazon CloudWatch insights based on source IP addresses.

B. Run an Amazon Web Services Cost and Usage report and sort the results by instance ID.

C. Send traffic to Amazon QuickSight using the VPC traffic mirroring feature.

D. For each individual instance, use Amazon CloudWatch measurements supplied by the NAT gateway.

125. A SysOps Administrator observed that Amazon CloudWatch reports 12,345,678 items in an S3 bucket, yet the AWS CLI reports 98,765,432 objects in the same bucket during an audit. Which Amazon S3 function can the SysOps Administrator utilize to get an accurate count of the objects in the bucket?

A. Amazon S3 analytics

B. Inventory on Amazon S3

C. Amazon Web Services Management Console

D. Tags for objects

126. While uploading data to one of their S3 buckets, an organization experienced a network disruption. In one S3 bucket, there were several incomplete multipart uploads as a result of the outage. A sysops administrator wishes to delete the incomplete multipart uploads and ensure that they are destroyed automatically the next time something similar happens. How should this be accomplished?

A. Set up an Amazon S3 Event Notification to send an AWS Lambda function to discard incomplete multipart uploads.

B. Create an Amazon S3 lifecycle rule to abort incomplete multipart uploads now and in the future, ensuring that they are removed.

C. Using the AWS CLI, create a list of all multipart uploads and abort all incomplete uploads from the event day so that they are deleted.

D. Abort all incomplete uploads from the day of the event using the AWS Management Console so that they are destroyed.

127. A company's finance department requests a monthly report detailing the use of AWS resources by department. To achieve the requirements, which solution should be used?

A. For each department, configure AWS Cost and Usage reports. Run the reports on a monthly basis.

B. Using AWS Budgets, create a monthly report for each department.

C. Create a monthly AWS CloudTrail report that shows resource utilization by tag and department code.

D. Assign department codes to all resources. Create a cost allocation report on a monthly basis.

128. A SysOps Administrator manages a number of Amazon EC2 instances that don't have public internet access. The instances require outbound internet connectivity to patch operating systems. The instances should not be accessible from the public Internet for security reasons. The Administrator sets up a NAT instance, updates the security groups, and configures the route table with the required routes. The instances, however, are still unable to connect to the Internet. What should be done to address the problem?

A. Create a route from the private subnets to the internet gateway by assigning Elastic IP addresses to the instances.

B. Replace the NAT instance with an Amazon Web Services WAF.

C. Disable source/destination checks on the NAT instance

D. Start/stop the NAT instance so it is launched on a different host
   C. Disable source/destination checks on the NAT instance

129. To comply with Information Security requirements, a SysOps Administrator utilizing AWS KMS must rotate all customer master keys (CMKs) every week. Which choice would be the most suitable for the task?

A. To manually cycle the encryption keys, create a new CMK every 7 days.

B. On the CMKs, enable key rotation and set the rotation period to 7 days.

C. Use AWS CloudHSM instead of AWS KMS because AWS KMS does not support key rotation.

D. To avoid having to rotate keys, use data keys for each encryption task.

130. In an Amazon EC2 Auto Scaling group, a SysOps Administrator manages an application that runs on Amazon EBS-backed Amazon EC2 instances. The program is set to kill unhealthy instances automatically. For future study, the Administrator wants to keep the application logs from these instances. What action will be taken to achieve this?

A. Switch from EBS to instance store as the storage type.

B. When the EC2 state changes to terminate, configure an Amazon CloudWatch Events rule to move the logs to Amazon S3.

C. Stream the logs to Amazon CloudWatch Logs using the unified CloudWatch agent.

D. Set up VPC Flow Logs for the subnet where the EC2 instance is located.

131. To prevent internet exposure, a SysOps Administrator must remove public IP addresses from all Amazon EC2 instances. Many corporate apps that run on those EC2 instances, however, require access to Amazon S3 buckets. The Administrator is responsible for permitting EC2 instances to access the S3 buckets. Which options are available? (Select two.)

A. In the VPC where the EC2 instances are running, deploy a NAT gateway and configure the route tables accordingly.

B. Modify the network ACLs in the routes to connect to Amazon S3 with private IP addresses.

C. Modify the security groups on the EC2 instances that connect to Amazon S3 with private IP addresses in the routes.

D. Configure a virtual interface between the EC2 instances and the S3 buckets using AWS Direct Connect.

E. In the VPC where the EC2 instances are running, create a VPC endpoint and configure the route tables accordingly.

132. A company's application, which was running on Amazon EC2 Linux, recently collapsed due to a memory shortage. If this happens again, management wants to be notified. Which combination of steps will enable you to do this? (Select two.)

A. Create an Amazon CloudWatch dashboard to track the instance's memory usage over time.

B. Create a dashboard alarm that sends an Amazon SNS notification to the CIO when a threshold is exceeded.

C. Create a metric alarm that sends an Amazon SNS notification to the CIO when a threshold is exceeded.

D. Use the AWS Personal Health Dashboard to set an alarm that sends an Amazon SNS notification to the CIO when the machine runs out of memory.

E. Set up the Amazon CloudWatch agent on the instance to collect and push memory consumption metrics.

133. Access to dynamic bidding information in near-real time is required by a popular auctioning platform. At all times, the platform must be accessible. During the weekend auction, the existing Amazon RDS instance frequently hits 100% CPU use and cannot be scaled. A sysops administrator is considering Amazon ElastiCache to increase application performance, and has chosen Redis (cluster mode enabled) over Memcached. What motivates you to make this decision? (Select two.)

A. Data segmentation
B. Processing in multiple threads
C. Multi-AZ with automatic failover
D. Multi-region failover (automated)
E. Resharding in the cloud

134. For its calculations, a financial services organization uses distributed computing software to handle a fleet of 20 computers. The calculations are carried out by two control nodes and 18 worker nodes. When necessary, control nodes can start worker nodes automatically. At the moment, all nodes are on demand, and the worker nodes are used for about 4 hours each day. Which action combination will be the most cost-effective? (Select two.)

A. For the control nodes, use Dedicated Hosts.
B. For the control nodes, use Reserved Instances.
C. For the worker nodes, use Reserved Instances.
D. If Spot Instances are not available, use On-Demand Instances for the control nodes. E. For the worker nodes, use Spot Instances and On-Demand Instances if Spot is not available.

135. A sysops administrator must keep track of a fleet of Amazon EC2 Linux instances without the use of agents. As a monitoring tool, the sysops administrator selects Amazon CloudWatch. Given the limits, what metrics can be measured? (Select three.)

   A. CPU Utilization
   B. Disk Read Operations
   C. Memory Utilization
   D. Network Packets In
   E. Network Packets Dropped
   F. CPU Ready Time

136. For an application, a sysops administrator built up an Amazon ElastiCache for Memcached cluster. The application's latency increases as it's being tested. CPU Utilization is regularly above 95%, while FreeableMemory is consistently under 1 MB, according to Amazon CloudWatch data for the Memcached cluster. Which course of action will be most effective in resolving the issue?

   A. Set up ElastiCache to automatically scale the Memcached cluster. Set the CPUUtilization and FreeableMemory metrics as scaling triggers when CPUUtilization is greater than 75% and FreeableMemory is less than 10 MB.
   B. To disperse the workload, configure ElastiCache to read replicas for each Memcached node in different Availability Zones.
   C. Install an Application Load Balancer to divide the workload across the Memcached cluster nodes.
   D. Remove the Memcached cluster and replace it with a node type with more CPU and memory.

137. According to a security audit, the security groups in a VPC have ports 22 and 3389 accessible to everybody, posing a risk of instances being stopped or configurations being changed. Automation of remediation is required by a sysops administrator. What should the system administrator do to ensure that these requirements are met?

A. Create an IAM controlled policy to prevent any security groups in a VPC from accessing ports 22 and 3389.

B. Using AWS Systems Manager automation documentation, define an AWS Config rule and a remediation action.

C. Use AWS Trusted Advisor to fix public port access issues.

D. To fix public port access, use AWS Systems Manager configuration compliance.

138. A company recently switched to Amazon Inspector from a third-party security program. For some Amazon EC2 instances, a list of security discoveries is missing, according to a sysops administrator. What action will you take to solve this issue?

A. Log in to the impacted EC2 instances and perform CLI instructions to manually generate the missing security findings list.

B. Log in to the EC2 instances that are affected. On each instance, download and install the Amazon Inspector agent from the AWS Marketplace.

C. Analyze network configurations with a network reachability package to find security vulnerabilities on the affected EC2 instances.

D. Make sure the Amazon Inspector agent is up and running on the impacted instances. The Amazon Inspector agent should be restarted.

139. A medical imaging company requires the use of a certain instance type to process massive amounts of imaging data in real time. The corporation wants to ensure that it has enough resources for a year. Which activity will be the most cost-effective in meeting these requirements?

A. Make 1-year On-Demand Capacity Reservations in the Availability Zones of your choice.

B. Create Amazon EC2 instances that have termination protection turned on.

C. Purchase Reserved Instances in the specific Availability Zones for a one-year period.

D. Combine numerous Availability Zones with a Spot Fleet.

140. A sysops administrator is attempting to use the AWS Management Console to start a new Amazon EC2 instance, however the instance is not launching. What could be the source of this issue? (Select two.)

A. The Region's EC2 limits have been reached on the AWS account.

B. The AWS account's EC2 limits for the Availability Zone have been reached.

C. There is no EC2 key pair specified.

D. An instance profile with ec2:RunInstances permissions is lacking from the EC2 instance.

E. There are no more usable private IP addresses on the subnet.

141. A corporation wishes to improve its auditing and compliance skills by dividing accounts across different teams. AWS Organizations are used to manage the accounts. Management wishes to give the security team secure access to the account logs while preventing them from being edited. How can a SysOps administrator do this with the FEASTEST possible operational overhead?

   A. In each account, save AWS CloudTrail logs in Amazon S3. Create a new account to hold compliance data and copy the items into it.

   B. In each account, store AWS CloudTrail logs in Amazon S3. Create a CloudTrail logs IAM user with read-only access.

   C. Using AWS CloudTrail, generate an organization trail from the master account and apply it to all Regions. To restrict access, use IAM roles.

   D. Create an AWS CloudTrail trail in each account using an AWS CloudFormation stack set and restrict rights to edit the logs.

142. A highly regulated corporation just transferred an Amazon EC2-based application to AWS. All network traffic data between the servers must be captured and stored for compliance purposes. Which solution requires the LEAST amount of effort to complete?

   A. On the VPC, install AWS CloudTrail. Assign the destination to Amazon CloudWatch Logs.

   B. On the VPC, install AWS CloudTrail. Assign the destination to Amazon S3.

   C. Create flow logs at the level of the elastic network interface. Assign the destination to Amazon S3.

   D. At the VPC level, create flow logs. Assign the destination to Amazon S3.

143. A business is extending its use of Amazon Web Services (AWS) across its several portfolios. To ensure a separation of business

activities for security, compliance, and billing, the organization intends to create AWS accounts for each team. Account creation and bootstrapping should be done in a scalable and efficient manner, with a clear baseline and governance guardrails in place. A SysOps administrator must devise a provisioning method that is both time and resource efficient. What steps should be made to attain these objectives?

A. Automate the provisioning of AWS accounts, infrastructure setup, and integration with AWS Organizations using AWS Elastic Beanstalk.

B. To provide accounts and infrastructure, create bootstrapping scripts in AWS OpsWorks and combine them with AWS CloudFormation templates.

C. Using AWS Service Catalog and AWS Config, provision accounts and deploy instances.

D. Create a template in Account Factory using AWS Control Tower and utilize the template to provide new accounts.

144. A company's online application has been suffering performance issues on a regular basis throughout the night. On an Amazon EC2 Linux instance, a root cause analysis showed spikes in CPU consumption that lasted 5 minutes. The goal of a SysOps administrator is to locate the process ID (PID) of the service or process that is using the most CPU. What is the most efficient way for the administrator to accomplish this?

A. Set up an AWS Lambda function in Python 3.7 to record the PID and deliver a notice every minute.

B. Set up the procstat plugin to gather and send CPU measurements for the processes that are currently running.

C. Each night, log in to the EC2 Linux instance with a.pem key and run the top command.

D. In the CloudWatch dashboard, capture the PID using the default Amazon CloudWatch CPU utilization statistic.

145. In a production context, a company is employing an Amazon ElastiCache for Redis cluster. A SysOps administrator must choose a
deployment that meets the company's technical requirements and
provides greater availability and fault tolerance. To achieve this
goal, what action should the SysOps administrator take?

   A. Create an ElastiCache cluster with Memcached as the cache
      engine.
   B. Use an Auto Scaling group to deploy the Redis cluster and
      launch replicas across various Availability Zones.
   C. Make sure cluster mode is turned off. Increase the quantity of
      shards in your game.
   D. Make sure Multi-AZ with automatic failover is turned on.
      Create several replicas in different Availability Zones.

146. An organization's chief financial officer (CFO) has seen an increase
in Amazon S3 storage expenses in recent months. These charges,
according to a SysOps administrator, are attributable to the storage
of earlier versions of S3 objects from one of the company's S3 buckets. What can the administrator do if this suspicion is confirmed?

   A. Enable Amazon S3 inventory and then query it to find out
      how much space previous object versions have used up.
   B. Identify the entire storage of prior object versions using
      object-level cost allocation tags.
   C. For the bucket, enable the Amazon S3 analytics functionality
      to determine the total storage of prior object versions.
   D. Determine the total storage of prior object versions using
      Amazon CloudWatch storage metrics for the S3 bucket.

147. In different VPCs, a corporation runs over 1,000 Amazon EC2
instances running Amazon Linux 2. On all EC2 instances, a Sys-
Ops administrator must alter the statically defined DNS server
IP address. Which option will necessitate the LEAST amount of
time and effort?

A. Create an AWS Lambda function to change all EC2 instances' corporate DNS IP addresses.

B. On each EC2 instance, run a shell script to update the corporate DNS IP address.

C. Configure the revised corporate DNS IP address in the Amazon Machine Images (AMIs) of the EC2 instances.

D. Update the corporate DNS IP address on all EC2 instances using the AWS Systems Manager Run Command.

148. A business wishes to save money on works that can be finished at any moment. Currently, numerous On-Demand Instances are used to perform the jobs, which take little under 2 hours to finish. A job can be restarted from the beginning if it fails for any reason. Based on these criteria, which method is the MOST cost-effective?

A. Get Reserved Instances for job execution.

B. Submit a one-time Spot Instance request for job execution.

C. Make a request for a Spot block, which will be used to execute the operation.

D. For job execution, use a mix of On-Demand and Spot Instances.

149. A corporation has a multi-account AWS system with the following components: All IAM users and groups are stored in a central identity account. IAM roles are present in several member accounts. Permissions for a specific IAM group to adopt a role in one of the member accounts must be granted by a SysOps administrator. What is the best way for the SysOps administrator to complete this task?

A. In the member account, add sts:AssumeRole permissions to the role's policy. In the identity account, add a trust policy to the group that specifies the account number of the member account.

B. In the member account, add the group Amazon Resource Name (ARN) to the role's trust policy. In the identity account, add an inline policy to the group with sts:AssumeRole permissions.

C. In the member account, add the group Amazon Resource Name (ARN) to the role's trust policy. In the identity account, add an inline policy to the group with sts:PassRole permissions.

D. In the member account, add the group Amazon Resource Name (ARN) to the role's inline policy. In the identity account, add a trust policy to the group with sts:AssumeRole permissions.

150. On AWS Lambda, an image processing system runs asynchronously. When an image fails to execute after three attempts, a SysOps administrator configures a Lambda function to inform developers. To notify the developers, the SysOps administrator generated an Amazon Simple Notification Service (Amazon SNS) topic. To achieve this criteria, what additional steps should the SysOps administrator take?

A. Set up an Amazon CloudWatch alarm for Lambda function problems, which will notify the Amazon SNS topic.

B. Create a dead-letter queue with the Amazon SNS topic as the target.

C. Before exiting, modify the Lambda function code to post failed orders to the Amazon SNS topic.

D. Use the AWS Personal Health Dashboard to sign up for Lambda function error notifications.

151. A SysOps administrator is looking into why a user has been unable to access to a bastion server operating on an Amazon EC2 Windows instance through RDP from their home PC. Which of the following could be the source of the problem? (Select two.)

A. The network traffic is being blocked by a network ACL connected with the bastion's subnet.

B. There is no private IP address assigned to the instance.

C. There is no route to the internet gateway in the route table associated with the bastion's subnet.

D. There is no inbound rule on port 22 in the instance's security group.

E. There is no outbound rule on port 3389 in the instance's security group.

152. A business is in charge of a website with a global user base that is hosted on Amazon EC2 and uses an Application Load Balancer (ALB). A SysOps administrator configures an Amazon Cloud-Front distribution with the ALB as the origin to lessen the burden on the web servers. After a week of monitoring the solution, the administrator finds that the ALB is still serving requests and that the web server load has not changed. What could be the source of this issue? (Select two.)

A. The ALB is not configured as the origin access identity in CloudFront.

B. Instead of pointing to the CloudFront distribution, the DNS is still pointing to the ALB.

C. CloudFront inbound traffic is blocked by the ALB security group.

D. On the CloudFront distribution, the default, minimum, and maximum Time to Live (TTL) are all set to 0 seconds.

E. Sticky sessions are enabled for the target groups associated with the ALB.

153. AWS Organizations are used by an organization to manage several AWS accounts. One of these accounts is just for the purpose of storing logs in an Amazon S3 bucket. The company wants to make sure that the account's computational resources aren't used. How can this be done with the FEASTEST administrative effort possible?

A. Create an IAM policy that clearly denies NotAction: s3:* to all IAM entities in the account.

B. Use AWS Config to terminate computing resources created in the accounts.

C. Set up AWS CloudTrail to prevent any action with an event source other than s3:amazonaws.com.

D. Update the account's service control policy to prevent unapproved services from being used.

154. A business is weighing options for connecting its data centers to a VPC in an AWS Region that is hosting a mission-critical application. As a catastrophe recovery solution, a secondary Region has already been built up. The company requires a reliable, low-latency connection with a minimum bandwidth of 10 Gbps that is also highly resilient and fault tolerant. Which solution satisfies these criteria?

A. Create two AWS Direct Connect connections, each capable of 10 Gbps. Use two customer routers and active/active connections that are dynamically routed.

B. Create an AWS Direct Connect connection with a speed of 10 Gbps. To support both regions, use a Direct Connect gateway.

C. Create an AWS Direct Connect connection to the VPC as the primary connection, and an AWSmanaged VPN connection as a backup.

D. Connect to the VPC via 10 VPN connections. To balance traffic across active connections, enable the VPN Equal Cost Multipath (ECMP) function.

76

155. According to a company's security policy, connecting to Amazon EC2 instances via SSH and RDP is not permitted. Authorized workers can connect to instances using AWS Systems Manager Session Manager if access is required. Users report being unable to connect to an Amazon EC2 instance running Ubuntu and pre-installed with the AWS Systems Manager Agent (SSM Agent). These users can connect to other instances in the same subnet using Session Manager, and they are members of an IAM group that has Session Manager access for all instances. What can a SysOps administrator do to fix this problem?

A. In the security group connected with the Ubuntu instance, add an incoming rule for port 22.

B. Add the AmazonSSMManagedInstanceCore managed policy to the Ubuntu instance's EC2 instance profile.

C. Set up the SSM Agent to use the login "ubuntu" to log in.

D. Create a new key pair, configure Session Manager to use it, and present the users with the private key.

156. To address concerns regarding high availability for an on-premises website, a SysOps administrator is considering Amazon Route 53 DNS possibilities. There are two servers that make up the website: a primary active server and a secondary passive server. If the linked health check returns 2xx or 3xx HTTP codes, Route 53 should send traffic to the primary server. The secondary passive server should receive all other traffic. Both primary and secondary servers have the required failover record type, set ID, and routing policy. What should be the next step in configuring Route 53?

A. For each server, create an A record. Associate the records with the HTTP health check for Route 53.

B. For each server, create an A record. Connect the documents to the Route 53 TCP health check.

C. For each server, create an alias record with evaluate target health set to yes. Associate the records with the HTTP health check for Route 53.

D. For each server, create an alias record with evaluate target health set to yes. Connect the documents to the Route 53 TCP health check.

157. A three-tier stateful web application is used by a firm. An Amazon CloudFront distribution with default setup options and an Application Load Balancer (ALB) as the origin serves the application. Users that are logged in are occasionally logged out and view inconsistent material. What should the organization do to provide a consistent user experience throughout a session?

A. On the ALB, enable session affinity (sticky sessions). Set up CloudFront to send all cookies to the origin server.

B. In CloudFront, limit viewer access to signed cookies. On the ALB, enable session affinity (sticky sessions).

C. On the ALB, switch from session affinity based on length (sticky sessions) to application-controlled session affinity (sticky sessions).

D. Set the CloudFront TTL to be equal to or less than the duration of the ALB session.

158. A company's application is hosted on two Amazon EC2 instances, each in a distinct Availability Zone. Both contain data that is crucial to the company's operations. Backups must be kept for seven days and updated every twelve hours. Which method requires the LEAST amount of effort to achieve these requirements?

A. Create snapshots of Amazon Elastic Block Store (Amazon EBS) volumes using an Amazon EventBridge (Amazon CloudWatch Events) scheduled rule.

B. Create a snapshot lifecycle policy for both instances using Amazon Data Lifecycle Manager (Amazon DLM).

C. Generate automated snapshots of Amazon Elastic Block Store (Amazon EBS) volumes using a batch process.

D. To copy the data to Amazon S3 Glacier, create an AWS Lambda function.

159. An application is being re-architected by a SysOps administrator. To restrict access from the public network, the SysOps administrator moved the database from a public subnet to a private subnet, where it used a public endpoint. An AWS Lambda function that requires read access to the database will no longer be able to connect to the database after this change. This issue must be resolved without jeopardizing security, according to the SysOps administrator. Which solution satisfies these criteria?

A. For the Lambda function, create an AWS PrivateLink interface endpoint. Use the database's private endpoint to connect to it.

B. Establish a connection between the Lambda function and the database VPC. Use the database's private endpoint to connect to it.

C. Assign an IAM role to the Lambda function that has database read access.

D. Transfer the database to a public network. For secure access, use security groups.

160. AWS has warned a company that hosts a multi-tier ecommerce web application to suspicious application traffic. Behind an Application Load Balancer, the architecture comprises of Amazon EC2 instances deployed across several Availability Zones (ALB). A SysOps administrator determines that the strange traffic is an attempted SQL injection attack after reviewing the instance logs. What should the SysOps administrator do to avoid future attacks like this?

A. Assign the ALB as the origin of an Amazon CloudFront distribution. To protect against SQL injection attacks at edge sites, enable AWS Shield Advanced.

B. Create an AWS WAF web ACL and a SQL injection rule to include in the web ACL. Associate the ALB with the WAF web ACL.

C. Turn Amazon GuardDuty on. When GuardDuty detects SQL injection, use Amazon EventBridge (Amazon CloudWatch Events) to activate an AWS Lambda function.

D. Configure a rules package in Amazon Inspector and install it on the EC2 instances. To discover and prevent SQL injection attacks, use the results reports.

161. A business is moving its exchange server from its on-premises location to an AWS VPC. Users who work from home connect to the exchange server via an encrypted, secure route via the internet. Users, on the other hand, are having problems receiving email since the switch to AWS. The following is seen in the VPC flow log data.

What is the problem's root cause?

A. An outbound network ACL banned SMTP transmission from the network interface.

B. An outbound security group banned SMTP communication from the network interface.

C. An incoming network ACL blocked SMTP traffic to the network interface.

D. An inbound security group prohibited SMTP transmission to the network interface.

162. A secondary Amazon Elastic Block Store (EBS) volume tied to an Amazon EC2 instance contains sensitive data. A new company policy mandates that the secondary volume be encrypted while in transit. Which solution will be able to achieve this criterion?

A. Take a copy of the volume as a snapshot. Create a new volume with the Encrypted parameter set to true from the snapshot. Remove the existing volume and replace it with the new volume.

B. Create an Amazon Machine Image (AMI) of the EC2 instance that is encrypted. Use the encrypted AMI to start a new instance. The original instance should be terminated.

C. Shut down the Amazon EC2 instance. AWS CloudHSM is used to encrypt the volume. Begin the instance and double-check the encryption.

D. Shut off the Amazon EC2 instance. Set the Encrypted parameter to true in the instance properties. Begin the instance and double-check the encryption.

163. An Amazon EC2 web server, an Amazon ElastiCache cluster communicating on port 6379, and an Amazon RDS for PostgreSQL DB instance communicating on port 5432 were recently established by a SysOps administrator. The web servers are in the web-sg security group, the ElastiCache cluster is in the cache-sg security group, and the database instance is in the database-sg security group. The application crashes when it tries to connect to the database, with the error message "Unable to connect to the database." The following are the web-sg rules.

Which update to web-sg should the SysOps administrator make to fix the problem without jeopardizing security?

A. Create a database-sg TCP 5432 inbound rule.
B. Create a database-sg TCP 5432 outbound rule.
C. Create a new outgoing rule: 0.0.0.0/0 0-65535 All Traffic
D. Replace cache-sg TCP 5432 with cache-sg TCP 5432 in the outbound rule.

164. AWS Linux has received a kernel patch, and computers must be updated to the latest version. A SysOps administrator must do an in-place update on an Amazon EC2 instance rather than replacing it. How should the instance's SysOps administrator apply the updated software version?

A. Using AWS Systems Manager Patch Manager, add the instance to a patch group and patch baseline containing the desired patch.
B. Create a new Amazon Machine Image for the instance (AMI). To the instance, apply the new AMI.
C. Create a new user data script with the patch in it. Use the new script to configure the instance.
D. Use the AWS CLI to remotely run commands on the instance.

165. A corporation needs to develop a write-once, read-many (WORM) object-based storage system. Objects can't be deleted or altered once they've been stored, not even by the root user or administrators of an AWS account. Which solution will be able to meet these demands?

A. Run daily updates on Amazon S3 Cross-Region Replication.
B. Enable S3 Versioning in Amazon S3 Object Lock in governance mode.
C. Enable S3 Versioning in Amazon S3 Object Lock in compliance mode.

D. To migrate the objects to Amazon S3 Glacier, create an Amazon S3 Lifecycle policy.

166. In the us-east-1 Region, a corporation runs a multi-tier web application with two Amazon EC2 instances in one Availability Zone. One of the EC2 instances must be moved to a new Availability Zone by a SysOps administrator. Which solution will be the most effective in achieving this goal?

A. Move the EC2 instance to a different Availability Zone on Amazon Web Services. The original instance should be terminated.

B. From the EC2 instance, create an Amazon Machine Image (AMI) and start it in a new Availability Zone. The original instance should be terminated.

C. Using the AWS CLI, move the EC2 instance to a different Availability Zone.

D. Shut down the EC2 instance, change the Availability Zone, and restart it.

167. AWS CloudFormation was used to deploy a company's application infrastructure, which consists of Amazon EC2 instances behind an Application Load Balancer. The instances are distributed across several Availability Zones in an EC2 Auto Scaling group. The update deployment must avoid DNS changes and allow rollback when publishing a new version of the application. Which option should a SysOps administrator utilize to meet the new release's deployment requirements?

A. Use lifecycle hooks in the Auto Scaling group and deploy new instances with the new application version. Once you're healed, finish the lifecycle hook action.

B. Make a new Amazon Machine Image (AMI) with the changed code in it. With the AMI, create a launch configuration. To use the new launch configuration, update the Auto Scaling group.

C. Create a second CloudFormation stack and deploy it. Wait for the app to become accessible. Replace the old Application Load Balancer with the new Application Load Balancer.

D. Add an AutoScalingReplacingUpdate policy to the Cloud-Formation template. Refresh the stack. Using the new release, run a second update.

168 A corporation wishes to establish a cluster of Amazon EC2 instances that must communicate with one another as quickly as feasible. When launching these instances, which actions should a SysOps administrator take? (Select two.)

A. Use a VPN tunnel to launch instances in various VPCs.

B. Use VPC peering to launch instances in different VPCs.

C. Create a cluster placement group and launch instances in it.

D. Create a spread placement group and launch instances in it.

E. Start instances that support enhanced networking.

169. A company may have many Amazon Web Services (AWS) accounts. AWS Organizations are used by the company, with one organizational unit (OU) for the production account and another for the development account. Developers are only allowed to use approved AWS services in the production account, according to corporate standards. What is the MOST OPERATINGLY EFFECTIVE way to manage the production account?

A. In AWS Identity and Access Management, create a customer-managed policy (IAM). The policy should be applied to all users in the production account.

B. In AWS Identity and Access Management, create a job function policy (IAM). Within the production OU, apply the policy to all users.

C. Make a policy for service control (SCP). The SCP should be applied to the production OU.

D. Make an Identity and Access Management (IAM) policy. To restrict the production account, use the policy in Amazon API Gateway.

170. AWS Lambda is used to connect with other AWS services, such as AWS Step Functions, Amazon DynamoDB, and Amazon S3, in a company's data processing workflow. As part of the workflow, the Lambda functions make various API calls to these services. In the AWS Region, AWS CloudTrail has been enabled and is logging to Amazon CloudWatch Logs. CloudWatch Logs are also used by Lambda functions. A SysOps administrator finds that a particular Lambda function in the workflow is taking longer to run than it was the previous month. The SysOps administrator must figure out which components of the Lambda function are taking longer than usual to respond. What is the best way to achieve this?

A. Look through CloudWatch Logs for the timestamps of API calls made while the Lambda function is running. Compare this month's logs to the prior month's logs.

B. For the function, enable AWS X-Ray. Analyze the service map and traces to find API calls that have unusual response times.

C. Look through the CloudTrail logs for Lambda function calls. Examine the observed and expected times of API calls in relation to the function's start time.

D. For the Lambda function, use CloudWatch to track the Duration metric of function invocations. Compare the results to the previous month's measurements.

171. IAM access keys are used by developers to manage AWS resources via the AWS CLI. When an access key has been in use for more than 90 days, the company policy mandates that it be disabled automatically. Which solution will be the most effective in achieving this goal?

A. Set up an Amazon CloudWatch alarm to activate an AWS Lambda code that disables keys that have been active for more than 90 days.

B. Set up AWS Trusted Advisor to detect and disable keys that are more than 90 days old.

C. Create a password policy for the account that expires in 90 days.

D. Identify noncompliant keys using an AWS Config rule. For remediation, create a custom AWS Systems Manager Automation document.

172. A corporation wants to use Amazon S3 to store sensitive data. Only the on-premises corporate network should have access to the S3 bucket and its contents. To configure the S3 bucket policy statement, what should a SysOps administrator do?

A. Use a Deny effect with an aws:sourceVpc key-based condition.

B. Use a Deny effect with a NotIpAddress key-based condition.

C. Use an Allow effect with an IpAddress key-based condition.

D. Create a condition based on the s3:LocationConstraint key and use an Allow effect.

173. A SysOps administrator wishes to use AWS Key Management Service to encrypt an existing Amazon RDS DB instance (AWS KMS). How should the SysOps administrator go about achieving this objective?

A. Copy the unencrypted instance's data volumes. Apply the KMS key to the data volumes that have been copied. With the encrypted volumes, start the instance.

B. Make an unencrypted read duplicate of the encrypted instance. Use the KMS key to encrypt the read replica. The read replica should be promoted to the primary instance.

C. Take a picture of the instance that isn't encrypted. Using the modify-db-instance command, apply the KMS key to the existing instance. Restart the instance if necessary.

D. Take a picture of the instance that isn't encrypted. Using the KMS key, create an encrypted copy of the snapshot. Restore the encrypted snapshot of the instance.

174. A company needs to deploy a web application behind an Application Load Balancer on two Amazon EC2 instances (ALB). The database will be hosted on two EC2 instances as well. The infrastructure must be configured for high availability across Availability Zones (AZs) and public access to instances must be limited as much as possible. What is the best way to accomplish this within a VPC?

A. Create a public subnet for the Application Load Balancer in each AZ, a private subnet for the web servers in each AZ, and a private subnet for the database servers in each AZ.

B. Create a public subnet for the Application Load Balancer in each AZ, a public subnet for the web servers in each AZ, and a public subnet for the database servers in each AZ.

C. Create one public subnet for the Application Load Balancer, a private subnet for the web servers in each AZ, and a public subnet for the database servers in each AZ.

D. Create one public subnet for the Application Load Balancer, a public subnet for the web servers in each AZ, and a private subnet for the database servers in each AZ.

175. A SysOps administrator is in charge of managing an Amazon EC2 instance fleet. The build artifacts are uploaded to a third-party service by these EC2 instances. The third-party service recently instituted severe IP whitelisting, requiring that all build uploads originate from a single IP address. What changes to the existing build fleet should the systems administrator make to meet this new requirement?

   A. Put all of the EC2 instances behind a NAT gateway and give the service the gateway IP address.
   B. Place all EC2 instances behind an internet gateway and give the service the gateway IP address.
   C. Combine all EC2 instances into a single Availability Zone and give the service the Availability Zone IP address.
   D. Move all of the EC2 instances to a peering VPC and give the service the VPC IP address.

176. An AWS CloudFormation template that provisioned Amazon EC2 instances, an Elastic Load Balancer, and Amazon RDS instances is managed by a SysOps administrator. CloudFormation stacks are created and deleted on a regular basis as part of a transformation project. After a stack has been destroyed, the administrator must guarantee that the RDS instances continue to execute. What steps should be made to attain these objectives?

   A. Remove the RDS resources from the template and update the stack.
   B. On the stack, enable termination protection.
   C. In the template, set the DeletionPolicy property for RDS resources to Retain.
   D. On RDS resources, set the deletion-protection setting.

177. For its production environment, a streaming corporation uses AWS resources in the us-east-1 Region. The streaming site's web tier is hosted on Amazon EC2 instances and is protected by an

Application Load Balancer (ALB). The instances are distributed across several Availability Zones in an EC2 Auto Scaling group. When the CPU utilization of the instances exceeds 75%, the Auto Scaling group is configured to scale. The user database is stored in an Amazon S3 bucket, and the video content is stored in an Amazon RDS MySQL cluster. According to Amazon Cloud-Watch measurements, the RDS MySQL Multi-AZ DB instance has roughly 16 GB of free RAM and a CPU utilization of 70%. Accessing the streaming page takes several seconds slower for people in Asia. Which combination of measures will reduce the time it takes for the access to load? (Select two.)

A. Set up RDS MySQL Multi-AZ to disperse queries over different Availability Zones and reduce RDS CPU and RAM use.

B. Modify the EC2 Auto Scaling group such that when CPU utilization reaches 50%, it scales horizontally.

C. In the Asia Pacific Region, set up a second production environment and use an ALB to distribute cross-Region access.

D. Create a second production environment in the Asia Pacific Region and route traffic using Amazon Route 53 latency-based routing.

E. Create an Amazon CloudFront distribution to manage static content for users in various geographical areas.

178. A large corporation may have many AWS accounts, one for each department. A SysOps administrator must assist the organization in lowering overhead and better managing its AWS resources. The SysOps administrator must also make sure that department users, including AWS account root users, have access to only the AWS services they need to do their jobs. Which solution will be able to meet these demands?

A. Make AWS Directory Service available. To restrict access, use Group Policy Objects (GPOs) on each department.

B. Consolidate all of the accounts into a single account. Make IAM groups for each department with only the permissions that are required.

C. Use AWS Organizations and service control policies (SCPs) to guarantee that accounts only use AWS services that are absolutely necessary.

D. Set up AWS Single Sign-On and restrict access to only the most important AWS services.

179. In a VPC, a security officer has ordered that internet access be disabled for subnets. Internet-bound traffic is currently routed across the subnets to a NAT gateway. While allowing access to Amazon S3, a SysOps administrator must delete this access. Which solution will be able to meet these demands?

A. Create a gateway to the internet. To utilize the internet gateway to transport traffic to Amazon S3, update the route table on the subnets.

B. Create an endpoint for an S3 VPC gateway. Update the route tables on the subnets to direct traffic to Amazon S3 via the gateway endpoint.

C. In each Availability Zone, create additional NAT gateways. To route traffic to Amazon S3, update the route table on the subnets to use the NAT gateways.

D. Create an internet gateway that only allows egress. To route traffic to Amazon S3, update the route table on the subnets to use the egress only internet gateway.

180. An application is running on Amazon EC2 instances, with all data being stored in Amazon S3. To save money, the corporation intends to archive all files older than 30 days. Archived files are only used for auditing, however the audit team may need to recover files in less than a minute. How does the SysOps administrator go about putting these criteria into action?

A. Create a policy in S3 to migrate all objects older than 30 days to S3 Standard-Infrequent Access (S3 Standard-IA).

B. Make a lifecycle rule that sends all items older than 30 days to S3 Glacier.

C. Create a lifecycle rule for all objects older than 30 days to be moved to S3 Standard-Infrequent Access (S3 Standard-IA).

D. Move files older than 30 days to S3 Glacier Deep Archive using S3 Intelligent-Tiering.

181. A corporation has created a new memory-intensive application that has been distributed across an Amazon EC2 Linux fleet. Because the organization is concerned about memory depletion, the development team wishes to use Amazon CloudWatch to track memory utilization. What is the MOST OPERATINGLY EFFEC-TIVE method of achieving this goal?

A. Create an AWS Lambda function to monitor the EC2 instances' memory usage. Amazon EventBridge can be used to schedule the Lambda function (Amazon CloudWatch Events).

B. Deploy the application on EC2 instances that are memory opti-mized. Use the MemoryUtilization statistic in CloudWatch.

C. To collect and submit metrics to CloudWatch, install the CloudWatch agent on the EC2 instances.

D. To collect and submit metrics to CloudWatch, install the CloudWatch monitoring scripts on the EC2 instances.

182. A corporation uses LDAP-based credentials and employs a SAML 2.0 identity provider. A SysOps administrator has set up multiple federated roles in a new AWS account to give groups of users who utilize LDAP-based credentials access to the AWS Management Console. Several groups wish to automate daily tasks using the AWS CLI on their desktops. The SysOps administrator has designed an application that authenticates a user and generates a SAML assertion to enable them to do so. To retrieve credentials for federated programmatic access, which API call should be used?

    A. sts:AssumeRoleAssumeRoleAssumeRoleAssumeRoleAs

    B. sts:AssumeRoleWithSAML sts:AssumeRoleWithSAML sts:Assume

    C. sts:AssumeRoleWithWebIdentity sts:AssumeRoleWithWebIdentity sts:AssumeRo

    D. sts:GetFederationToken D. sts:GetFederationToken

183. As part of an application's continuous integration/continuous delivery (CI/CD) process, a SysOps administrator implements automated I/O load performance testing. For each instance that is restored from a snapshot, the application uses an Amazon Elastic Block Store (Amazon EBS) Provisioned IOPS volume and requires consistent I/O performance. The I/O performance results are irregular during the initial tests. The SysOps administrator must guarantee that the outcomes of the tests are more consistent. What steps could a SysOps administrator take to achieve this goal? (Select two.)

    A. With rapid snapshot restore enabled, restore the EBS volume from the snapshot.

    B. Using the cold HDD volume type, restore the EBS volume from the snapshot.

    C. Restore the EBS volume from the snapshot and read all of the blocks to pre-warm the volume.

D. Configure encryption and restore the EBS volume from the snapshot.

E. Restore the EBS volume from the backup and set the I/O block size to a random value.

184. A three-tier web application is hosted on Amazon EC2 instances in an Auto Scaling group behind an Application Load Balancer for a streaming services company (ALB). When the Auto Scaling group scales in, there is a deregistration delay, which can be greater than the time it takes to end an EC2 instance. Before the EC2 instance is terminated, a SysOps administrator must guarantee that the most recent logs are transferred to an external system. Which solution will be the most effective in resolving this issue?

A. To place the EC2 instance in a wait state until the log files are delivered, add a lifecycle hook to the Auto Scaling group.

B. Set up a fixed response for the ALB to utilize custom error messages instead of HTTP error response codes to respond to incoming requests.

C. For the Auto Scaling group, create an Amazon CloudWatch alarm based on the RequestCountPerTarget statistic. Wait until the EC2 instance is terminated before modifying the cooling period.

D. Update the launch settings to enable Auto Scaling group scale-in protection and remove the EC2 instance protected for termination.

185. A SysOps administrator must use IP addresses to register targets for a Network Load Balancer (NLB). To accomplish this task, which prerequisites should the SysOps administrator check?

A. Select ELBSecurityPolicy-TLS-1-2-Ext-2018-06, ELB-SecurityPolicy-FS-1-2-Res-2019-08, or ELBSecurityPolicy-TLS-1-0-2015-04 as the NLB listener security policy.

B. Make sure the Matcher configuration's health check setting on the NLB is between 200 and 399.

C. Verify that the targets are in one of the following CIDR blocks: 10.0.0.0/8 (RFC 1918), 100.64.0.0/10 (RFC 6598), 172.16.0.0/12 (RFC 1918), or 192.168.0.0/16 (RFC 1918). (RFC 1918).

D. Before registering the targets using IP addresses, make sure the NLB is exposed as an endpoint service.

186. A corporation has a web application that is hosted in a virtual private cloud (VPC). This web application's inbound traffic is routed through an internet gateway to a Network Load Balancer (NLB). The traffic is then routed over two private subnets to several Amazon EC2 machines. In order to detect potential hacking efforts, the organization intends to do deep packet inspection on inbound traffic. Which solution satisfies these criteria?

A. Set up AWS Shield in the VPC.

B. On the VPC, use AWS Network Firewall. Deep packet inspection should be enabled in Network Firewall.

C. On the subnets, use AWS Network Firewall. Deep packet inspection should be enabled in Network Firewall.

D. Set up Traffic Mirroring on one of the NLB's inbound ports.

187. In front of a pair of private web servers in multiple Availability Zones, a SysOps administrator has put up a new public Application Load Balancer (ALB). User traffic now goes to one web server only after deploying an updated AWS CloudFormation template with several changes. What is the MOST LIKELY cause of the traffic imbalance between the two servers?

A. The problematic server was removed since it was returning HTTP 200 codes.

B. For the working server, sticky sessions have been disabled in the ALB.

C. The ALB is using a custom ping path that the malfunctioning server does not support.

D. HTTP/2 is used by the web clients, and it is terminated at the ALB.

188. Users of a company's AWS account are launching Amazon EC2 instances without the cost allocation tags that are required. In AWS Organizations, a SysOps administrator must restrict users from starting new EC2 instances without the proper tags. The solution must have the smallest operating overhead possible. Which solution satisfies these criteria?

   A. Create an AWS Lambda function to trigger a run instance event and check for required tags. If the tags are absent, configure the function to prohibit EC2 instances from being launched.

   B. Create an AWS Config rule to keep an eye on EC2 instances that are missing the required tags.

   C. Create a service control policy (SCP) that forbids EC2 instances from being launched without the requisite tags. Connect the SCP to the root of the organization.

   D. Create an Amazon CloudWatch alarm to prevent any EC2 instances from running without the proper tags.

189. A business recently moved its three-tier web application to Amazon Web Services (AWS). The application is deployed on Amazon EC2 instances in an Auto Scaling group. At 1-minute intervals, a SysOps administrator must develop a monitoring dashboard to track CPU and network consumption for each instance. What is the best way for a SysOps administrator to achieve this requirement?

   A. Create a basic monitoring dashboard for Amazon CloudWatch.

   B. Create an Amazon QuickSight dashboard for AWS CloudTrail.

   C. Create a dashboard in Amazon CloudWatch and activate detailed monitoring.

   D. Make use of the Amazon Web Services Personal Health Dashboard.

190. A corporation uses Amazon EC2 Linux instances in public sub-nets in a VPC to host backend web services. A SysOps admin-istrator attempts to connect to the instance through SSH but is unsuccessful. What could have caused the connection to fail?

    A. Inbound traffic on port 22 is not allowed by the security group.
    B. Outbound traffic on port 80 is not allowed by the network ACL.
    C. Outbound communication on port 3389 is not allowed by the security group.
    D. Inbound traffic on port 443, according to the network ACL, is not allowed.

191. A business utilizes a large number of Amazon Elastic Block Store (Amazon EBS) volumes. Amazon Data Lifecycle Manager (Ama-zon DLM) will be used to manage the lifecycle of EBS snapshots with the tags "Production" and "Compliance." To activate this function, you'll need to do which of the following? (Select two.)

    A. A 5 GB minimum storage requirement
    B. One IAM role for Amazon DLM and another for users.
    C. Encryption of EBS volumes
    D. 3 IOPS/GB as a minimal baseline performance
    E. Tagging of the EBS volumes

192. of the EBS is tagged. A business is developing a record-keeping program. The program will operate on Amazon EC2 instances and will store its data in an Amazon Aurora MySQL database. To remain compliant, the application must not keep information that has been identified as sensitive. Which method should a Sys-Ops administrator employ to determine whether sensitive data is stored in the application?

A. Use an AWS Lambda function to export data from the database. Amazon S3 is a great place to save your data. Examine the stored data with Amazon Macie. Examine the report for any potentially sensitive information.

B. Download and install the Amazon GuardDuty Aurora plugin. Set up GuardDuty to look at the database. In GuardDuty, add the necessary EC2 CIDR ranges to the trusted IP list. Examine the report for any potentially sensitive information.

C. Install the Amazon Inspector agent on all EC2 instances to deploy Amazon Inspector. Set the assessment type of Amazon Inspector to HOST assessment. With the Aurora DB cluster, include NETWORK communications. Examine the report for any potentially sensitive information.

D. Examine communication between the EC2 instances and the Aurora DB cluster using VPC Flow Logs. Amazon S3 is a great place to keep log files. Examine the extracted log files with Amazon Detective. Examine the report for any potentially sensitive information.

193. Within a VPC, a SysOps administrator need a secure connection to AWS Key Management Service (AWS KMS). Connections to AWS KMS must not go across the internet, according to the SysOps administrator. What is the SAFEST option that fits these criteria?

   A. Connect to AWS KMS via a bastion host.

   B. Connect to AWS KMS using a NAT gateway.

   C. To connect to AWS KMS, use a VPC gateway endpoint for Amazon S3.

   D. To connect to AWS KMS, use a VPC interface endpoint.

194. A corporation wants to use Amazon EC2 for numerous business units. All business units will be required to provide their EC2 instances using only approved EC2 instance configurations, according to the corporation. What should a SysOps administrator do to put this need into action?

A. Create a launch configuration for an EC2 instance. By providing this launch configuration in the AWS Management Console, the business units will be able to launch EC2 instances.

B. Create an IAM policy that restricts business units to only provisioning EC2 instances. Instruct the business units to use an AWS CloudFormation template to launch instances.

C. Using AWS Service Catalog, publish a product and launch a constraint role for EC2 instances. Allow only AWS Service Catalog activities to be performed by business units.

D. Provide the business units with an AWS CloudFormation template. To allow AWS CloudFormation to manage EC2 instances, instruct the business units to pass a role to the service.

195. A company's application is hosted on an Amazon EC2 instance in one of its Availability Zones. The program must be highly available, according to a SysOps administrator. From the operating EC2 instance, the SysOps administrator has prepared a launch configuration. A load balancer has also been appropriately configured by the SysOps administrator. What is the next step for the SysOps administrator to make the application highly available?

A. Use the launch configuration to create an Auto Scaling group that spans at least two Availability Zones. Set the minimum capacity to one, the desired capacity to one, and the maximum capacity to one.

B. Use the launch configuration to create an Auto Scaling group that spans at least three Availability Zones. Set the minimum capacity to two, the desired capacity to two, and the maximum capacity to two.

C. Use the launch configuration to create an Auto Scaling group that spans at least two AWS Regions. Set the minimum capacity to one, the desired capacity to one, and the maximum capacity to one.

D. Use the launch configuration to create an Auto Scaling group that spans at least three AWS Regions. Set the minimum capacity to two, the desired capacity to two, and the maximum capacity to two.

196. A SysOps administrator is putting a new batch process through its paces. Every day, the batch job will upload 20 GB of data to an Amazon S3 bucket from Amazon EC2 instances in a private subnet. A little fee is reported when the first test is completed. "NAT Gateway – Data Processed" is the title of the fee. What can the SysOps administrator do to reduce the cost of future tests?

A. Create a VPC endpoint and use it.

B. Create an S3 bucket policy to ensure that the uploads are encrypted in transit.

C. Select the S3 Intelligent-Tiering storage class for the S3 bucket.

D. For the S3 bucket, disable cross-origin resource sharing (CORS).

197. In an Amazon VPC, a SysOps administrator is deploying a fleet of over 100 Amazon EC2 instances. A new DNS server must be added to the instances after they have been set up and are serving clients for DNS resolution. What is the most cost-effective method of making this change?

A. Make changes to the Amazon VPC's DHCP parameters.

B. Update the DNS server configuration for each instance using AWS OpsWorks.

C. Update the DMS server configuration for each instance using AWS Systems Manager.

D. Create a script to update each instance's DNS server configuration.

198. A corporation wishes to keep track of Amazon EC2 use costs based on the value of a Business-Unit tag. Developers are instructed by company leaders to update all EC2 resources with the tag. The developers inform the leaders that this assignment has been finished. A member of the finance team examines Cost Explorer later that week. The member of the finance team notices EC2 costs in various accounts but is unable to locate the Business-Unit tag to filter or group by. What is the most plausible cause for the absence of the Business-Unit tag?

A. In the AWS Billing and Cost Management console, the Business-Unit tag is not active as a cost allocation tag.

B. The Business-Unit tag is invalid since dashes are not allowed in tag key names (-).

C. The instances were restarted, but the developers forgot to re-add the Business-Unit tag thereafter.

D. In Cost Explorer, the IAM user does not have access to read the tags.

199. A developer designed a new application that makes use of Spot Fleet to manage many instance families across several Availability Zones. What should the developer do to make sure the Spot Fleet is set up to save money?

A. Deploy a capacityOptimized allocation strategy for provisioning Spot Instances.

B. Ensure instance capacity by providing the target capacity and the percentage of that capacity that must be On-Demand.

C. In the Spot Fleet request, use the lowestPrice allocation technique with InstancePoolsToUseCount.

D. Launch instances up to the maximum permissible payment amount or the Spot Fleet target capacity.

200. To resolve an issue, a SysOps administrator must run a script on production servers. All remote interactive access to production servers is prohibited per company policy. How should the administrator run the script in this situation?

A. To acquire access to the servers and run the script, share and use the Amazon EC2 key pairs.

B. Insert the script into the instances' user data.

C. On the EC2 instances, set up the script to execute as a cron job or a scheduled task.

D. Run the script with AWS Systems Manager.

201. A corporation hosts a website on an Amazon EC2 instance that is part of a VPC's public subnet. For web server log analysis, the organization uses Amazon CloudWatch Logs. On the EC2 instance, a SysOps administrator installed and configured the CloudWatch Logs agent and verified that it was operating. Logs, on the other hand, do not appear in CloudWatch Logs. Which approach will be the most effective in resolving this problem?

A. Change the security group rules for the EC2 instance to allow inbound traffic on port 80.

B. Create a CloudWatch logs IAM user with the appropriate capabilities. Create an IAM instance profile and link it to a user in IAM. Associate the EC2 instance with the instance profile.

C. Create an IAM role with the required CloudWatch log rights. Create an IAM instance profile and link it to the appropriate IAM role. Associate the EC2 instance with the instance profile.

D. Change the public subnet's network ACL rules in the VPC to allow inbound traffic on port 80.

202. Users have been modifying cost-related tags on Amazon EC2 instances after deployment, according to a corporate audit. The corporation has an AWS Organization with a large number of AWS accounts. The organization need a solution that would automatically discover EC2 instances. The solution must have the smallest operating overhead possible. Which solution satisfies these criteria?

   A. Track EC2 instances that do not have the requisite tags using service control policies (SCPs).

   B. Run a report with Amazon Inspector to find EC2 instances that don't have the needed tags.

   C. Track EC2 instances that don't have the requisite tags with an AWS Config rule.

   D. Run a report using the AWS Well-Architected Tool (AWS WA Tool) to detect EC2 instances that lack the appropriate tags.

203. A company discovers that many of their gp2 Amazon EBS volumes are running out of space.

   Which solution will cause the LEAST amount of disturbance with the least amount of effort?

   A. Create a snapshot and restore it to a large gp2 volume

   B. Create a RAID 0 with another new gp2 volume to increase capacity

   C. Leverage the elastic volumes feature of EBS to increase gp2 volume size

   D. Write a script to migrate data to a larger gp2 volume

204. For disaster recovery purposes, a corporation intends to expand into other AWS Regions. AWS Cloudformation is used by the company, and its infrastructure is well-defined as code. When deploying resources to new locations, the corporation wants to utilize as much of its existing code as feasible.

A SysOps Administrator is looking at how AMIs are chosen in AWS Cloudformation, but is having problems getting the same stack to function in a different area. Which action would make managing many Regions easier?

A. Name each AMI in the new region precisely the same as the corresponding AMI in the previous region.

B. Duplicate the stack so that unique AMI names can be coded into the appreciate stack.

C. Create an alias for each AMI so that it can be referenced by a common name across regions.

D. In the stack, create a Mappings section and define the Region to AMI associations.

205. The expected system logs are not being received by cloudwatch logs after installing and configuring the Amazon Cloudwatch agent on an EC2 instance. Which of the following is most likely to be the source of this issue? (CHOOSE TWO)

A. For logs, a special third-party solution is employed.

B. The IAM role associated with the EC2 instance lacks the necessary permissions.

C. The cloudwatch agent does not work with the current operating system.

D. This account's quantity of cloudwatch logs is limited due to a billing constraint.

E. The EC2 instance is on a private subnet with no NAT gateway in the VPC.

206. A web application is being developed for access to a fleet of Amazon EC2 instances, which requires a consistent view of persistent data. The things kept range in size from 1KB to 300MB, and they are often read, generated, and frequently require partial changes without causing conflict. The data will not exceed 2TB, and things will be expired based on their age and content kind. Which AWS services fit these criteria?

    A. An Amazon S3 bucket with lifecycle controls in place to ensure that old objects are deleted.

    B. Amazon RDS PostgreSQL with a task that deletes ROWS depending on the age and file type fields.

    C. Amazon EFS with a scheduled deletion mechanism depending on file age and extension

    D. An Amazon EC2 instance storage that is synced from a central Amazon EBS-backed instance when it boots up.

207. An organization is concerned about a security flaw in their Linux operating system. What can the SysOps Administrator do to address this issue?

    A. Use Amazon Inspector to patch the flaw.

    B. Provide the AWS Trusted Advisor report showing which Amazon EC2 instances have been patched

    C. Redeploy the Amazon EC2 instances using Amazon Web Services Cloudformation.

    D. Using AWS system management, patch the Linux operating system.

208. In one Availability Zone, a company's application is operating on an EC2 instance. The application's high availability has been assigned to a SysOps Administrator. From the operating EC2 instance, the administrator prepared a launch configuration. A load balancer was also appropriately configured by the administrator.

What is the next action for the administrator to do to ensure that the application is highly available?

A. Create an Autoscaling group by using the launch configuration across at least two availability zones with a minimum size of one, desired capacity of one, and a maximum size of one

B. Create an Autoscaling group by using the launch configuration across at least three availability zones with a minimum size of two, desired capacity of two, and a maximum size of two

C. Create an Autoscaling group with a minimum size of 1, desired capacity of 1, and maximum size of 1 utilizing the launch configuration across at least 2 regions.

D. Create an Autoscaling group with a minimum size of 2, intended capacity of 2, and maximum size of 2 utilizing the launch configuration across at least 2 regions.

209. An examination of the AWS environment is being conducted by the company's IT security team to determine which servers need to be patched and where additional security should be introduced. Which of the following is the company's responsibility? (CHOOSE TWO)

A. Patching Amazon RDS instances' operating systems

B. Patching Amazon EC2 instances' operating systems

C. Enabling server-side encryption on S3 objects using Amazon S3-Managed Keys (SSE-S3)

D. Patching RDS instances' database engines

E. Elastic beanstalk controlled EC2 application patching

210. The Infosec team has requested that the company's Amazon RDS database instances be hardened by the SysOps Administrator. What activities should be proposed for the start of the security evaluation based on the requirement? (Choose TWO)

   A. Use Amazon Inspector to generate a detailed report of security vulnerabilities in the RDS database fleet.
   B. Check the security group incoming access rules for least privilege.
   C. Export all SSH activity on the RDS instances as AWS cloudtrail entries.
   D. On each RDS instance, use the cat command to enumerate the allowed SSH keys in /.ssh.
   E. Check the VPC settings and make sure that encrypted connections are enabled.

211. A SysOps administrator must break down a team's single AWS Cloudformation template into smaller, service-specific templates. A single, shared Amazon S3 bucket is referenced by all of the services in the template. What should the Administrator do to ensure that all service templates can reference this S3 bucket?

   A. Include the s3 bucket as a mapping in each template
   B. Add the S3 bucket as a resource in each template
   C. Create the S3 bucket in its own template and export it
   D. Generate the S3 bucket using StackSets.

212. Behind an ELB Application Load Balancer, a Company web application runs on Amazon EC2 instances. The EC2 instances are distributed across several Availability Zones in an EC2 auto scaling group. An Amazon Elastic Cache for Redis cluster and an Amazon RDS DB instance store the data. All system patches must be completed by Tuesday midnight, according to company policy. Which resources will require a maintenance window set for Tuesday at midnight? (Choose TWO)

A. Elastic Load Balancer

B. EC2 instances

C. RDS database instances

D. ElastiCache Cluster

E. Auto Scaling Group

213. With the AWS root account user, a Sysops administrator must validate that security best practices are being followed. What steps should the Administrator take to make sure this is done?

A. Change the root user password on a regular basis using the AWS CLI.

B. Use the AWS CLI to rotate the root user's access keys and secret keys on a regular basis

C. Use AWS Trusted Advisor security checks to assess the root user's configuration

D. Distribute the AWS compliance document from AWS Artifact that governs the root user's configuration on a regular basis

214. A SysOps Administrator must give data demonstrating the overall consumption of Amazon EC2 instances within each department, as well as determining whether the Reserved instances ordered are being used successfully. What service should you utilize to get the information you need?

A. Amazon Web Services Personal Health Dashboard

B. Amazon Web Services Cost Explorer

C. Amazon Web Services Service Catalog

D. Amazon Web Services Application Discovery Service

215. A Sysops Administrator builds a customer gateway resource in AWS while setting up an AWS managed VPN connection. The customer gateway device is housed in a data center and is protected by a Nat gateway. To construct a customer gateway resource, what address should be used?

A. The customer gateway device's private IP address

B. The NAT device's Mac address in front of the customer gateway device

C. The customer gateway device's public IP address

D. The NAT device's public IP address in front of the customer gateway device

216. A SysOps Administrator has set up a Cloudwatch agent to send custom metrics to Amazon Cloudwatch and is now putting together a Cloudwatch dashboard to display them. How should the Administrator go about completing this task?

A. Select the Amazon Web Services Namespace filter by metric name then add to the dashboard

B. Add a text widget, select the appropriate metric from the custom namespace then add to the dashboard

C. Select the appropriate widget and metrics from the custom namespace then add to the dashboard

D. Open the CloudWatch console, from the CloudWatch Events, add all custom metrics.

217. Several important data were recently accidentally destroyed from a shared Amazon S3 bucket. By enabling MFA Delete, a SysOps Administrator was tasked with preventing future mistakes. Which bucket activities will require MFA authentication once MFA is enabled? (SELECT TWO)

A. Permanently removing an object version from the bucket

B. Disabling the bucket's default object encryption

C. Listing all versions of removed objects in the bucket

D. Suspending versioning on the bucket

E. Enable Multi-Factor Authentication (MFA). Add bucket

218. to the mix. An organizational audit revealed an existing Amazon RDS database that is not currently setup for high availability; it must be configured as soon as possible. What is the best way to meet this requirement?

    A. Use the create-db-instance-read-replica command with the –availability-zone argument to establish an active/passive database pair.

    B. When building a new RDS instance, specify high availability and live-migrate the data.

    C. Modify the RDS instance using the console to include the Multi-AZ option.

    D. Use the -ha flag

219. with the modify-db-instance command. A VPC has been built in an AWS account by the networking team. The application team has requested access to other account resources. The VPC peering connection between the two accounts has been setup by the SysOps Administrator, but resources in one VPC cannot connect to resources in the other VPC. What could be the source of this problem?

    A. One of the VPCs is not properly sized for peering.

    B. One of the VPCs does not have a public subnet.

    C. The route table has not been updated.

    D. One of the VPCs has disabled the peering flag.

220. A System Administrator is in charge of keeping a company's custom, approved AMIs up to date. Other AWS accounts must be able to use the AMIs. What is the best way for the Administrator to deal with this problem?

A. To share AMIs with other AWS accounts, contact AWS support.

B. Make the AMIs publicly accessible by modifying their permissions.

C. Make the IAM Role that is linked with the AMI publicly accessible by modifying its permissions.

D. Using the console or CLI

221, share the AMIs with each AWS account. Billing updates should be sent out more frequently than once a month, according to the Accounting Department. They want to use a spreadsheet program to keep track of the updates. What is the best way to satisfy this request?

A. Schedule a billing enquiry every two weeks using Amazon Cloudwatch events. To convert the output to CSV, use AWS Glue.

B. Use AWS Cost and Usage reports to publish invoices in CSV format to an Amazon S3 bucket on a daily basis.

C. Output billing data as JSON using the AWS CLI. Use Amazon SES to email bills on a daily basis

D. Use AWS Lambda to query billing data and push to Amazon RDS

222, which is triggered by cloudwatch. A SysOps Administrator must create a report that breaks down every API activity by a specific user during the course of a single call API operation. How can this report be generated now that AWS Cloudtrail has been enabled?

A. Search for the user name in the Cloudtrail history using the AWS management console. The report can then be filtered by API and downloaded in CSV format.

B. Use the company's Amazon S3 bucket to store cloudtrail digest files. Then, to create the report, send the log to Amazon QuickSight.

C. Look for the cloudtrail monthly reports that are emailed to the account root users. Then, using a secure channel, send the reports to the auditor.

D. Obtain access to Cloudtrail logs stored in an Amazon S3 bucket. Extract the data needed to create the report using Amazon Athena.

223. Which AWS service can show up resources are affected when the AWS Cloud Infrastructure experiences an event that may have an impact on an organization?

A. Amazon Web Service Health Dashboard

B. Amazon Web Service Trusted Advisor

C. Amazon Web Service Personal Health Dashboard

D. Amazon Web Service Systems Manager

224. On an EC2 instance, a corporation is hosting a social media site. To boost read times, the application stores data in an Amazon RDS for MySQL cluster and stores read caching in an Elastic Cache for Redis (cluster mode enabled) cluster. A social event is approaching, and SysOps Administrator anticipates a threefold increase in website traffic. What can a SysOps Administrator do to ensure that users' read times during the social event are improved?

A. Take advantage of Amazon RDS Multi-AZ.

B. Add shards to the Redis Cluster that already exists.

C. Use Amazon S3 to store static data.

D. Create a second Redis Cluster

225. with multiple AZs. In Amazon ElasticCache, a SysOps Administrator is in charge of a MemCached cluster. With a large instance type with additional memory, the cluster was ready for capacity. What method should the Administrator employ in order to make this change?

   A. Use the ModifyCacheCluster API and specify a new CacheNodeType

   B. Use the CreateCacheCluster API and specify a new CacheNodeType

   C. Use the ModifyCacheParameterGroup API and specify a new CacheNodeType

   D. Use the RebootCacheCluster API and specify a new CacheNodeType

226. A company's website is hosted on Amazon EC2 instances that are protected by an Application Load Balancer. The company wants to point the apex of its domain zone to the website. To achieve these requirements, what form of record should be used?

   A. An AAAA record for the domain zone Apex

   B. An A record for the domain zone Apex

   C. A CNAME record for the domain zone Apex

   D. An Alias Record for the domain zone Apex

227. A SysOps Administrator has established an AWS Direct Connect connection between an AWS account and a data center in region us-east-1. The Administrator must now link the data to a VPC in the us-west-2 AWS Region, which must have constant network performance and minimal latency. What is the MOST EFFECTIVE and FASTEST method of establishing this connection?

   A. Create an AWS VPN cloudhub architecture and connect to the VPC in region us-west-2 using software VPN.

   B. Establish a new Direct Connect link between the data center and the us-west-2 area.

C. Establish a VPC peering connection between the VPCs in regions us-east-1 and us-west-2, and connect to the VPC in region us-west-2 from the data center.

D. Use the Direct Connect gateway with the VPC's Virtual Private Gateway in region us-west-2, which already has a Direct Connect connection.

228. An Amazon Aurora DB cluster with an Aurora replica stores data for a web-commerce application. The application reads data from the reader endpoint to show shopping cart information. The AuroraReplicaLagMaximum metric for a single replica is high, according to the SysOps Administrator, who is monitoring the Aurora database. What is the most likely behavior that the app will display to users?

A. Users are unable to add any products to their shopping carts.

B. Users are immediately aware that the cart is not appropriately updated.

C. Users can't take anything out of their shopping cart.

D. Users are unable to use the application because it keeps reverting to an error page.

229. An Amazon EC2 link to the Internet is being investigated by a SysOps Administrator. The EC2 instance's private subnet is applied to the EC2 instance's subnet.

Destination – 10.2.0.0/16
Target – local
Status – Active
Propagated – No

Destination – 0.0.0.0/0
Target – nat-xxxxxx
Status – Blackhole
Propagated – No

What has caused the connectivity issue?

A. There is no longer a NAT gateway.

B. The Internet Gateway is not reachable.

C. The routes are no longer proliferating

D. There is no route rule with a destination for the internet

230. A recent change was made to an Amazon EBS Volume linked to an EC2 instance. Increased capacity was one of the changes made. The increased storage capacity is not reflected in the file system, as the administrator notices. To make use of the enhanced storage capacity, what should the Administrator do?

A. Restart the EC2 instance

B. Extend the volume file system

C. Detach, resize, and reattach the EBS volume

D. Take an EBS snapshot and restore it to the larger volume

231. During a security assessment, it was discovered that the web application hosted in an Amazon EC2 Instance is being targeted by a coordinated attack using incorrect HTTP headers. What AWS feature or service would block this traffic from reaching the EC instances?

A. Amazon Inspector

B. Security Group

C. Amazon Web Services WAF

D. Application Load Balancer

232. A SysOps Administrator gets told that a version of MySQL RDS database cluster has a security issue. Who is in charge of making sure the patch is installed on the MySQL cluster?

A. The database vendor

B. The security department of the SysOps Administrator company

C. Amazon Web Services

D. The SysOps Administrator

233. An Auto Scaling group with a step scaling policy has been deployed by a SysOps Administrator. The Administrator discovers that the aggregated metrics are missing the new instances. Why aren't the additional instances included in the totaled metrics?

A. The warm-up period has not expired

B. The instances are still in the boot process

C. The instances has not been attached to the auto scaling group

D. The instances are included in a different set of metrics

234. An InstanceLimitExceeded issue occurred while a SysOps Administrator was creating extra Amazon EC2 instances. What is the root of the problem, and how can it be fixed?

A. The administrator requested too many instances at once and must request fewer instances in batches.

B. The concurrent running instance limit has been surpassed, and an EC2 limit increase request must be submitted to AWS support.

C. Because AWS currently lacks sufficient capacity, an alternative instance type must be employed

D. When establishing EC2 instances

235 the Administrator must define the maximum number of instances to be created. All EC2 instances and Amazon Elastic Block Storage (EBS) volumes must be tagged, according to a SysOps Administrator's plan. What can the Administrator do to put this in place for real-time enforcement?

A. Use the AWS Tag Editor to manually search for untagged resources and then tag them properly in the editor

B. Set up an AWS Service Catalog rule with the TagOptions Library rule that enforces a tagging taxonomy proactively when instances and volumes are launched

C. Use the resource tagging GetResources API action in a power shell or shell script to check for untagged items and then manually tag the reported items.

D. Use the AWS API to launch objects. When the instances and volumes are deployed, use the TagResources API action to apply the required tags

236. Customers of a corporation are experiencing higher delay when viewing static web content stored on Amazon S3. On a specific S3 bucket, a SysOps Administrator noticed a very high rate of read operations. What can be done to reduce latency by reducing the load on the S3 bucket?

A. Move the S3 bucket to a region closer to the end users' physical locations.

B. Replicate all of the data to another region using cross-region replication.

C. Assign the S3 bucket as the origin of an Amazon Cloudfront distribution.

D. Cache data served from Amazon S3

237. using Amazon Elastic. An e-commerce company wants to reduce the cost of its nightly operations that aggregate the previous day's sales and save the data in Amazon S3. Currently, the jobs are executed utilizing numerous on-demand instances, and they take little under two hours to finish. A job must be restarted from the beginning if it fails for any reason. Based on these criteria, which method is the most cost-effective?

A. For job execution, use a combination of On-Demand and Spot instances.

B. Make a request for a Spot Block to be used to execute an operation.

C. Invest in a reserved instance for job execution.

D. Make a one-time spot instance request for job execution.

238. SSL is being implemented by a SysOps Administrator for a domain of an internet-facing application that is running behind an Application Load Balancer. To protect it, the Administrator chooses to utilize an SSL certificate from Amazon Certificate Manager (ACM). When attempting to create an ALB request, the error message "Domain not allowed" appears. What can the Administrator do to resolve the problem?

A. Contact the domain registrar and request that they give the AWS-required verification.

B. Instead of using the ALB FQDN, create a new request with a correct domain name.

C. In the ACM console, select the certificate request and resend the validation email.

D. Contact AWS customer service and confirm the request by answering security challenge questions.

239. Malicious traffic is making its way to the company's web servers. This traffic must be blocked by a SysOps Administrator. The fraudulent traffic request is addressed and represents significantly more traffic than what is generally seen from legitimate users. How should the web servers be protected by the Administrator?

A. Create a web server security group and add refuse rules for dangerous sources.

B. Add deny entries to the network access control list for the web servers subnet.

C. Use AWS WAF to protect a web server and set a rate limit to generate a blacklist.

D. Cache all pages on Amazon Cloudfront to eliminate traffic from the web servers.

240. An Amazon VPC with an IPV6 CIDR block was built by a Sys-Ops Administrator, and it requires internet access. However, access to VPC from the internet is forbidden. After you've added and configured all of the necessary components to the VPC. The Administrator is unable to connect to the internet from his private subnet. What extra route destination rules should be added to the route tables by the Administrator?

A. Use a NAT gateway to route::/0 traffic.

B. Send traffic to an Internet Gateway via::/0.

C. Forward 0.0.0.0 traffic to an internet gateway that only accepts egress traffic.

D. Send ::/0 traffic to an internet gateway that only accepts egress traffic.

241. A corporation is storing log data in Amazon S3 buckets using a centralized AWS account. Before uploading data to S3 buckets, a solutions architect must guarantee that the data is encrypted at rest. In addition, the data must be encrypted while in transit. Which solution satisfies these criteria?

A. Encrypt the data being uploaded to the S3 buckets using client-side encryption.

B. Encrypt the data being uploaded to the S3 buckets using server-side encryption.

C. For S3 uploads, create bucket policies that require server-side encryption with S3 managed encryption keys (SSE-S3).

D. Use a default AWS Key Management Service (AWS KMS) key to encrypt the S3 buckets by enabling the security option.

242. A company wants to use Amazon EC2 instances running Windows Server 2016 to create a shared file system for its .NET application servers and Microsoft SQL Server databases. The solution must work with the company's Active Directory domain, be extremely durable, be managed by AWS, and have high throughput and IOPS. Which solution meets these requirements?

A. For Windows File Server, use Amazon FSx.

B. Make use of Amazon's Elastic File System (AWS) (Amazon EFS).

C. Switch to file gateway mode on AWS Storage Gateway.

D. Deploy a Windows file server across two Availability Zones on two On Demand instances.

243. A company is preparing to create a data lake on AWS. A strategy for encrypting data at rest must be described by a solutions architect. S3/Amazon Keys must be rotated every 90 days, according to the company's security policy.

A clear line of demarcation between important users and key administrators must be established.

It must be feasible to audit key usage.

What are the solutions architect's recommendations?

A. Customer-controlled customer master keys with AWS KMS managed keys (SSE-KMS) (CMKs)

B. AWS KMS controlled keys (SSE-KMS) with AWS managed client master keys on the server side (CMKs)

C. Customer-controlled customer master keys with server-side encryption using Amazon S3 managed keys (SSE-S3) (CMKs)

D. AWS managed customer master keys with server-side encryption using Amazon S3 managed keys (SSE-S3) (CMKs)

244. A company uses Amazon Web Services to run a three-tier environment that collects sensor data from its customers' gadgets. The traffic is routed through a Network Load Balancer (NLB), then to Amazon EC2 instances for the web tier, and lastly to Amazon EC2 instances for the database layer. What can a solutions architect do to make data more secure when it's delivered to the web tier?

A. Set up a TLS listener on the NLB and add the server certificate.

B. On the NLB, configure AWS Shield Advanced and enable AWS WAF.

C. Convert the load balancer to an Application Load Balancer and connect it to AWS WAF.

D. Using the AWS Key Management Service, encrypt the Amazon Elastic Block Store (Amazon EBS) volume on the EC2 instances (AWS KMS).

245. A company wants to improve a hybrid application's availability and performance. The application consists of a stateful TCP-based workload hosted on Amazon EC2 instances in multiple AWS Regions and a stateless UOP-based job maintained on-premises. To improve availability and performance, what activities should a solutions architect combine? (Choose two.)

A. Use AWS Global Accelerator to create an accelerator. Assign endpoints to the load balancers.

B. Create an Amazon CloudFront distribution with an origin that routes requests to load balancers using Amazon Route 53 latency-based routing.

C. In each Region, set up two Application Load Balancers. The first will send traffic to EC2 endpoints, while the second will send traffic to on-premises endpoints.

D. In each Region, configure a Network Load Balancer to handle the EC2 endpoints. In each Region, configure a Network Load Balancer to route traffic to on-premises destinations.

E. In each Region, configure a Network Load Balancer to address the EC2 endpoints. In each Region, configure an Application Load Balancer to transport traffic to the on-premises endpoints.

246. A solutions architect checks the security of a recently moved workload. The workload is a web application made up of Amazon EC2 instances in an Auto Scaling group that are routed through an Application Load Balancer. The solutions architect must improve security and reduce the impact of a DDoS attack on resources. Which of the following is the MOST EFFECTIVE solution?

A. Create an AWS WAF ACL that includes rate-based rules. Create an Amazon CloudFront distribution with the Application Load Balancer as the destination. On the CloudFront distribution, enable the WAF ACL.

B. Create a custom AWS Lambda function that adds discovered assaults to a common vulnerability pool in order to detect a possible DDoS attack. Modify a network ACL to deny access using the discovered information.

C. Make VPC Flow Logs available and save them to Amazon S3. Create a custom AWS Lambda function that examines logs for DDoS attacks. Block identified source IP addresses by modifying a network ACL.

D. Configure Amazon GuardDuty to write findings to Amazon CloudWatch and enable Amazon GuardDuty. Create a CloudWatch Events event for DDoS alarms that sends an email to Amazon Simple Notification Service (Amazon SNS). Invoke a custom AWS Lambda function from Amazon SNS to scan the logs and check for a DDoS attack. Block identified source IP addresses by modifying a network ACL.

247. An ecommerce solution with a load-balanced front end, a container-based application, and a relational database is being developed by a company. A solutions architect must create a system that is highly accessible and requires minimal human intervention. Which options meet these requirements? (Choose two.)

A. Create a Multi-AZ Amazon RDS database instance.

B. In another Availability Zone, create an Amazon RDS DB instance and one or more replicas.

C. To accommodate the dynamic application load, set up an Amazon EC2 instance-based Docker cluster.

D. To accommodate the dynamic application load, create an Amazon Elastic Container Service (Amazon ECS) cluster with a Fargate launch type.

E. To handle the dynamic application load, create an Amazon Elastic Container Service (Amazon ECS) cluster with an Amazon EC2 launch type.

248. A company used Amazon EC2 in a single Availability Zone and an Amazon RDS Multi-AZ database instance to develop a stateless two-tier application. The organization's new leadership wants to make sure that the application is easy to use. What measures should a solutions architect do to meet this criterion?

A. Create an Application Load Balancer and configure the application to use Multi-AZ EC2 Auto Scaling.

B. Set the program to take EC2 instance snapshots and send them to a separate AWS Region.

C. Set up the application to leverage Amazon Route 53's latency-based routing to feed requests to it.

D. Create a Multi-AZ Application Load Balancer and configure Amazon Route 53 rules to handle incoming requests.

249. The administrator of a large corporation wants to keep an eye on and prevent cryptocurrency-related attacks on the company's AWS accounts. Which AWS service can be used by the administrator to protect the company from cyberattacks?

A. Amazon Cognito

B. Amazon GuardDuty

C. Amazon Inspector

D. Amazon Macie

250. An on-premises data center houses a company's data, which is used by a range of on-premises applications. The company wants to keep its current application infrastructure while adopting AWS services for data analytics and visualizations in the future. What kind of storage service should a solutions architect recommend to his or her customers?

A. Redshift of Amazon

B. Amazon Web Services Storage Gateway for files

C. Amazon EBS

D. Amazon EFS

SOLUTIONS

1. Answer: *C E*

2. Answer: *B*

3. Answer: *B*

4. Answer: *D*

5. Answer: *C*

6. Answer: *C D*

7. Answer: *A C*

8. Answer: *C*

9. Answer: *D*

10. Answer: *B*

11. Answer: *D*

12. Answer: *D*

13. Answer: *B*

14. Answer: *A*

15. Answer: *B*

16. Answer: *A*

17. Answer: *A*

18. Answer: *D*

19. Answer: *D*

20. Answer: *C*

21. Answer: *A*

22. Answer: *D*

23. Answer: *B*

24. Answer: *B*

25. Answer: *D*

26. Answer: *B*

27. Answer: *D*

28. Answer: *C D*

29. Answer: *D*

30. Answer: *D*

31. Answer: *C*

32. Answer: *C E*

33. Answer: *D*

34. Answer: *C*

35. Answer: *A*

36. Answer: *C*

37. Answer: *D*

38. Answer: *B*

39. Answer: *A E*

40. Answer: *B*

41. Answer: *D*

42. Answer: *C*

43. Answer: *D*

44. Answer: *D*

45. Answer: *C*

46. Answer: *B*

47. Answer: *C*

48. Answer: *B D*

49. Answer: *B*

50. Answer: *A C*

51. Answer: *B*

52. Answer: *C*

53. Answer: *D*

54. Answer: *D*

55. Answer: *A*

56. Answer: *A*

57. Answer: *C*

58. Answer: *B*

59. Answer: *A*

60. Answer: *B*

61. Answer: *D E*

62. Answer: *C*

63. Answer: *A*

64. Answer: *D*

65. Answer: *B*

66. Answer: *D*

67. Answer: *B*

68. Answer: *C*

69. Answer: *D*

70. Answer: *A C*

71. Answer: *C*

72. Answer: *D*

73. Answer: *A C*

74. Answer: *C*

75. Answer: *C*

76. Answer: *C*

77. Answer: *D*

78. Answer: *D E*

79. Answer: *A*

80. Answer: *D*

81. Answer: *D*

82. Answer: *D*

83. Answer: *A*

84. Answer: *B E*

85. Answer: *D*

86. Answer: *D*

87. Answer: *B*

88. Answer: *A*

89. Answer: *D*

90. Answer: *B*

91. Answer: *D*

92. Answer: *B*

93. Answer: *B*

94. Answer: *B*

95. Answer: *C*

96. Answer: *D*

97. Answer: *A*

98. Answer: *C*

99. Answer: *A*

100. Answer: *B*

101. Answer: *C*

102. Answer: *C*

103. Answer: *C*

104. Answer: *C*

105. Answer: *A*

106. Answer: *D*

107. Answer: *A*

108. Answer: *A*

109. Answer: *A*

110. Answer: *A*

111. Answer: *B*

112. Answer: *B*

113. Answer: *A*

114. Answer: *C*

115. Answer: *D*

116. Answer: *A*

117. Answer: *C*

118. Answer: *A*

119. Answer: *C*

120. Answer: *D*

121. Answer: *C*

122. Answer: *C*

123. Answer: *C*

124. Answer: *A*

125. Answer: *B*

126. Answer: *B*

127. Answer: *A*

128. Answer: *A*

129. Answer: *A*

130. Answer: *D*

131. Answer: *A E*

132. Answer: *A D*

133. Answer: *B C*

134. Answer: *C D*

135. Answer: *A B D*

136. Answer: *D*

137. Answer: *B*

138. Answer: *C*

139. Answer: *A*

140. Answer: *A D*

141. Answer: *C*

142. Answer: *D*

143. Answer: *A*

144. Answer: *B*

145. Answer: *D*

146. Answer: *D*

147. Answer: *D*

148. Answer: *C*

149. Answer: *A*

150. Answer: *A*

151. Answer: *C E*

152. Answer: *A B*

153. Answer: *D*

154. Answer: *B*

155. Answer: *A*

156. Answer: *C*

157. Answer: *C*

158. Answer: *A*

159. Answer: *D*

160. Answer: *A*

161. Answer: *C*

162. Answer: *A*

163. Answer: *A*

164. Answer: *A*

165. Answer: *B*

166. Answer: *B*

167. Answer: *A*

168. Answer: *C E*

169. Answer: *A*

170. Answer: *D*

171. Answer: *D*

172. Answer: *A*

173. Answer: *A*

174. Answer: *A*

175. Answer: *C*

176. Answer: *C*

177. Answer: *B C*

178. Answer: *A*

179. Answer: *C*

180. Answer: *A*

181. Answer: *D*

182. Answer: *B*

183. Answer: *A B*

184. Answer: *D*

185. Answer: *D*

186. Answer: *D*

187. Answer: *A*

188. Answer: *C*

189. Answer: *A*

190. Answer: *D*

191. Answer: *B E*

192. Answer: *A*

193. Answer: *B*

194. Answer: *C*

195. Answer: *B*

196. Answer: *A*

197. Answer: *A*

198. Answer: *A*

199. Answer: *B*

200. Answer: *C*

201. Answer: *B*

202. Answer: *A*

203. Answer: *C*

204. Answer: *D*

205. Answer: *B E*

206. Answer: *A*

207. Answer: *D*

208. Answer: *B*

209. Answer: *B C*

210. Answer: *B E*

211. Answer: *C*

212. Answer: *C D*

213. Answer: *C*

214. Answer: *B*

215. Answer: *D*

216. Answer: *C*

217. Answer: *A D*

218. Answer: *C*

219. Answer: *C*

220. Answer: *D*

221. Answer: *B*

222. Answer: *D*

223. Answer: *C*

224. Answer: *B*

225. Answer: *A*

226. Answer: *D*

227. Answer: *D*

228. Answer: *B*

229. Answer: *A*

230. Answer: *B*

231. Answer: *C*

232. Answer: *C*

233. Answer: *D*

234. Answer: *B*

235. Answer: *B*

236. Answer: *C*

237. Answer: *A*

238. Answer: *B*

239. Answer: *C*

240. Answer: *A*

241. Answer: *A*

242. Answer: *A*

243. Answer: *A*

244. Answer: *A*

245. Answer: *A D*

246. Answer: *A*

247. Answer: *A D*

248. Answer: *A*

249. Answer: *B*

250. Answer: *B*

www.ingramcontent.com/pod-product-compliance
Lightning Source LLC
LaVergne TN
LVHW051653050326
832903LV00032B/3782